A Sunset Book

Garden Art & Decoration

By the editorial staffs of
Sunset Books and Sunset Magazine

LANE BOOK COMPANY
Menlo Park, California

Contents

FIFTH PRINTING JULY 1964

Cover photographs. Mosaic tile, page 45; photo by Clyde Childress. Pottery and tiles, page 9; photo by Ernest Braun. Fence panel, page 31; photo by Clyde Childress.

ART IN

Your enjoyment of the garden or outdoor living area can be enhanced by the addition of a favorite piece of art work. The examples shown here are just a sampling of places where we've found an appreciation of art and a love of gardening happily combined.

Imaginative gardeners are finding many ways to use art in the garden—for its surprise quality, for enrichment, for a change in texture and form from garden foliage.

The property line fence which often demarcates the outdoor living area is an ideal wall from which to hang many types of garden decoration. If it is in full view through a glass wall of the house, you will want to choose something that is compatible with your interior decoration as well as its outdoor environment. Flat fence tops and brick or stone walls provide display space for some objects. In a garden bed, you may want to place a ceramic figurine or a planter. For a dramatic effect, a free-standing panel can be moved around as a backdrop for seasonal plant displays.

A garden gate is an ideal place for making a first impression. Your choice of decoration here can be a clue to the kind of life you live in the garden beyond. Screening devices can be decorative, in addition to serving as protection from the wind or sun.

To dramatize your garden in the evening, give it a focal point by spotlighting a special piece of

The Royal Family, a triumvirate of scrapwood statuary by Edward M. Brownlee, is focal point of entry garden.

Playful decorative panel for a
garden fence is made of
concrete, cast in sand mold.

THE GARDEN

art work. Sculpture in the round or deep bas relief is particularly effective when night lighting intensifies the patterns of highlights and shadows.

There are no rules for using art in the garden; it should be put where it gives you the greatest pleasure. There are certain factors, however, that must be considered for success. One is size. Depending on viewing distance and background, things usually must be in larger scale than they would be inside—particularly something that is to serve as a focal point. Smaller objects can be used for pleasant effects, of course; but in general, successful outdoor art is bold and simple.

The materials used in outdoor decoration must be able to withstand wind, rain, sun, and tempera-ture changes. Earth materials such as brick, clay, concrete, pebbles and stones, some metals, and natural wood blend best with garden foliage. Designers use these materials always with an eye to how they will look when weathered. Time and the elements usually bring a rich patina to woods and metal, and soften and fade the colors of clay, brick, and concrete.

You will probably want to change things around from time to time. Don't display too many unrelated elements in one place. The effect is confusing and prevents you from fully enjoying any one of them.

If you are adept at such crafts as ceramics, metal or wood working, or mosaics, you can make

The tops of walls and fences make good spots for displaying favorite pieces of pottery. These delightfully fanciful owls, which sit atop a brick garden wall, were done in clay by Kenneth Shores.

TOM BURNS, JR.

your own designs. If not, choosing a piece of garden decoration is an excellent way to acquaint yourself with the work of local artists. You can check with architects, landscape architects, and local craft centers or art schools for the names of people doing the type of work that you wish to feature in your garden.

On vacation trips, you are likely to find pieces that work perfectly in a garden display—small ceramic tiles from Sweden, North Africa, or Sicily, carved wood from the Orient, pottery bowls or vases from Mexico or from Vallauris in the south of France. You may come across something so exciting that you will decide to redesign your garden around the prized new possession!

Left. Strong focal point for quiet tree-shaded garden court is provided by stone sculpture on monolithic base. By Mark Sponenburgh.

RICHARD DAWSON

Clay planters come in all shapes and sizes. Here is a roguish red-clay figure with a hatful of succulents. Planter was designed and made by Mrs. Edmond Estey.

JEANETTE GROSSMAN

Bright-eyed birds done in copper by metal arts hobbyist, Mrs. E. S. Beach, are attached to stakes; can easily be moved to various locations in the garden.

Using a sheet of her own bubbled glass work, Mrs. C. M. Brink designed and made this bird feeder, which hangs from wisteria outside a breakfast room window.

An attractive plant displayed in a container can be an important part of your garden decoration. This Japanese black pine stands out boldly against dark wood panel.

Sparkling glass wind chimes are made from bits of stained glass (scraps from a glass store), glued to nylon fishing line threaded through weathered wood block.

A stage setting for plant displays, this free-standing wood carving and panel mount dramatically enhances a small corner of the terrace. By George Tsutakawa.

DARROW M. WATT

Concrete units to decorate a patio corner. Technique for making them is described on pages 22 and 23. Above planters contain a miniature landscape, a driftwood and sand arrangement, a rock and gravel pool.

Craft Projects for the Garden

To the creative person whose interests lie in the craft fields, the garden offers all kinds of possibilities for using his talents. A garden setting is an ideal background for hand-crafted objects; and a wonderful sense of achievement goes with the completion of a craft project that turns out successfully and becomes a permanent part of the garden scene.

There are projects for the craftsman all through this book—particularly in the chapters on fence decoration, garden pools, and decorative paving—but this chapter gathers together an inspiring group of single ideas that fall into the broad category of "garden crafts."

This is a "how-to" chapter. It includes projects that a beginner can complete with satisfaction in a few hours, and others for the more experienced craftsman. Ideas range from simple flower-pot wind bells to hang in the patio to a major undertaking like a mosaic bird bath. Materials, too, are varied, with some objects made of wood, and others of stone, tile, or concrete.

There are no rules for design in these projects. You can copy the designs exactly as they are shown here, or you can add your own variations; and once you have mastered the technique of a craft such as mosaic or sculpture, you will very likely want to apply that technique to designs that are entirely your own. Be as fanciful as you wish. One of the most intriguing aspects of making decorative objects for the garden is that you can let your imagination have free rein.

Garden bench is supported on colored drain tiles.

Left. Table is made of paving tiles 12 inches square, glazed and then fired. Tiles were then set on wood, grouted, enclosed in a 2 by 2-inch redwood frame. Hanging clay planters were formed in mold, then fired. Pots on bench in background were hand-thrown.

ERNEST BRAUN

POTTERY AND TILES

Pottery decorates this patio, bringing to it more than the usual quality of an outdoor "room," in transition between indoors and garden.

The handsome objects were made by ceramist Edith Heath. The table in the foreground uses glazed paving tiles. Glazes are painted on the tiles, then fired. The hanging planters are made from clay rolled out like pie crust and pressed by hand into a simple mold (use a salad bowl or a wooden or sand trough). Let clay dry for about a day, then remove, clean, and drill holes (4 for rope, 1 for drain). These are fired clay; they may also be glazed.

The objects shown were fired at a heavy clay products manufacturer's kiln. If you can find one in your locality, you may be able to have a batch fired at fairly low cost. However, the operator must either have his own glazes or run a test on those you put on, because ordinary pottery glazes

may lose their color at the temperatures of these kilns. You can also fire the objects at a ceramist's kiln, which you can locate through ceramics classes at adult education schools, ceramic supply shops, or potters' studios.

This same patio is shown in color on the front cover of this book. The square planter on the cover is made of 15-inch tiles decorated and glazed in the artist's kiln and dropped into place in a rabbeted redwood frame.

The bench above is also decorated with colored tiles. These tiles are 12 inches long, 5½ inches in outside diameter. They are loosely set now, but held in place by compression of vertical 2 by 8-inch wood supports. For greater stability, they will eventually be set in (or all or partly filled with) concrete, with bolts cast to hold the top.

Some other materials you might want to consider for glazing are flower pots, the clay dishes used under them, or even bricks.

ART HUPY

Pert cat of light vermiculite concrete has a stone-like texture and silvery, mica-flecked sparkle. Follow steps shown below to make stylized animals, birds, or other figures to adorn your garden. Cat pictured at left and below is by sculptor Del MacBride.

A SCULPTURED CAT

Sculpture is one of the easiest of the art crafts for a beginner to undertake successfully, and vermiculite concrete is one of the easiest sculptural media.

Mix used is 1 part of vermiculite, 1 of asbestos fiber (sold as "asbestos shorts" at some building materials stores), 1 of white sand, 1½ of white Portland cement, a little more than 1 of water. For color, add 1 teaspoon of cement pigment.

A mix of vermiculite, sand, and cement in a 1-1-1½ ratio is already easy to carve and sets slowly. The addition of 1 part asbestos fiber improves these characteristics.

Lime may irritate the skin, so use a hand lotion liberally before and after you work on the figure (or wear rubber gloves).

After curing, sand figure; then brush on 2 coats of silicone-base masonry water repellent.

1. Work from a preliminary study in clay (modeling clay or pottery clay with grog added) approximating the final larger figure.

2. Core for finished sculpture is made by nailing together short pieces of 2 by 4's, taking care to keep well within the final contours.

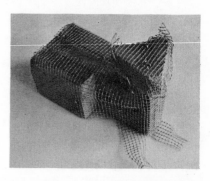

3. Cut hardware cloth with tinsnips; nail or staple it to form. Use pliers to bend it to round off corners and to reinforce or stiffen projecting parts.

4. Mix ingredients dry, in wheelbarrow for easy handling. When mixture is stiff enough to ball in your hands, start building it up on form.

5. Press mix on, adding or cutting back. Useful tools include small trowel, tablespoon, paring knife, spatula, and stiff palette knife.

6. Mix will set up in 24 hours, so you can still carve next day. To cure, cover with damp cloth and plastic sheet for 3 days; then air-dry 1 week.

Christmas roses, pine, and moss set off a white pottery figure of St. Francis in rustic garden shrine. A little soil or sand in base helps to keep greens fresh.

Shadow box shrine of finished lumber stained dark stands out against a split cedar fence. Evergreen and deciduous flowering shrubs and trees soften fence and frame shrine.

A GARDEN SHRINE

You can make a decorative garden shrine from slab cuts of cedar or fir with the bark left on, or from weathered wood—driftwood picked up at the beach, or silver-gray shakes from a deserted barn or mountain cabin. For a less rustic looking shrine, you can use scraps of finished lumber.

Scale the shrine to the figure you intend to display; tall and narrow for a slender figure, wider to include flowers and branches.

Place the shrine at eye level or a little lower, in much the same way you would hang a picture.

Small shrine is set among the trees in a corner of the garden. Simple triangular niche was built into a rough-sawn lumber framework to hold a gold-and-white plaster madonna by Mark Sponenburgh.

Weathered cedar fence post supports this shrine of split cedar. Bark roof adds to rustic look.

A few carefully chosen stones, embedded in a graceful pattern, in a small table-bench, make a patio showpiece, and the mosaic provides a safe resting place for hot dishes when you serve patio meals.

STONE MOSAIC IN A PATIO TABLE

A simple stone mosaic embedded in one end of this patio table-bench gives it special interest. And the stones serve more than a decorative purpose; they also form a resting place for hot dishes.

The bed for the mosaic was gouged out with a router (a power tool you adjust to cut to an exact depth), and a sharp wood chisel. If you can't find a router for rent or for sale (not all power tool companies or hardware stores stock them), you can do the whole job with the chisel.

This idea can be applied to almost any wooden table, and the mosaic can be made of other materials, such as mosaic glass tile. If you do not already have a table you want to decorate, the plan below gives construction details for the one shown in our photographs.

On the opposite page are step-by-step photographs showing how the mosaic was made. Design by Emmy Lou Packard.

Close-up of mosaic. Color shades were intensified by waxing stones, polishing with suede shoe brush.

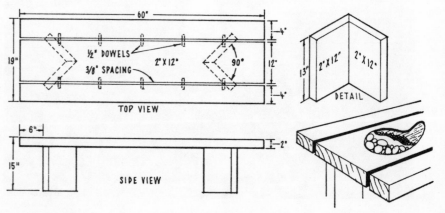

Table construction details. Note the simple and attractive way in which the redwood boards are joined for the table top: Drill ½-inch holes 1 inch deep in edges of the boards; join with ½-inch dowels, then glue.

1. Arrange stones as you want them, then transfer the pattern to heavy paper. Or arrange the stones right on the pattern paper, and then draw.

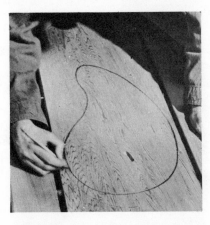

2. Cut the design for the mosaic out of the paper, then use a soft lead pencil to trace the design onto the surface of the table.

3. Begin cutting with router. Adjust depth of cut according to size of the rocks. If you use chisel instead of router, make sure it is sharp.

4. Chisel remaining wood in center of design, using flat strokes (the surface needn't be smooth). Keep edge as neat as you can.

5. Form a bed for each stone. Depth depends on size of rocks—test rocks as you work. If depths are correct, surface will be reasonably level.

6. Protect table with paper "mask," then apply wood sealer to bed. Wood screws between resting places for large stones help secure them.

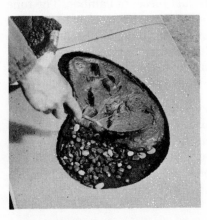

7. Spread gravel in thin layer. Mix grout (about 5 cups Portland cement and 3 cups sand for this mosaic). Add water until mixture is creamy.

8. Add larger stones, pushing and twisting them firmly into the grout until each is in place. This is your last chance to level the stones.

9. Place smaller stones between the larger ones, then push handfuls of gravel into grout. Rest of table can be finished in any way you prefer.

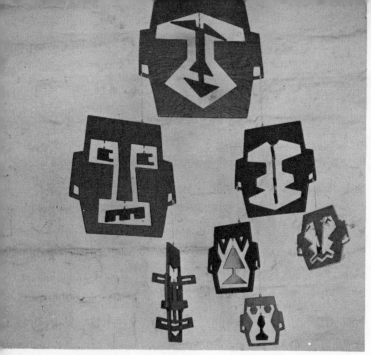

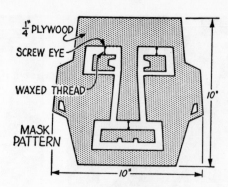

Pattern for large mask in group at left. Separate eye and mouth pieces are hung in the open areas.

For a whimsical bit of decoration, masks made of plywood are tied together to form this mobile. Hang it in front of a plain wall for the best effect.

MOBILE OF MASKS

These plywood masks are so simple to make that you might try some just to see how you like them. They vary in size from the 1-foot-square mask, top, to the 4-inch mask, lower right. At night the mobile casts moving shadow patterns on the wall.

Each mask is a flat face frame with one or more movable features that change position in response to air movements. They were cut out of ¼-inch plywood—with a brace and bit and a coping saw—and painted various contrasting colors.

The pieces are attached by means of small screw eyes and waxed linen thread. At first, better fasten on screw eyes temporarily with cellulose tape while you do some preliminary maneuvering to get the best grouping and balance.

Design: T. Newton Russell.

BAMBOO WIND CHIMES

Hang these chimes from a tree limb or a patio roof beam, and they'll strike together in the wind.

The chimes are just pieces of bamboo. The tone from each depends on the dimensions—the greater the diameter and length, the deeper the tone—so vary the sizes for a variety of tones. Cut each piece so that the bamboo joint closes the top but leave the bottom open for greater resonance.

Put a screw eye in each piece of bamboo and attach heavy cord. Or drill a hole through the joint or about an inch from the top, thread cord through the hole, and secure it with knots. The cord must be long enough to allow the bamboo lengths to swing freely. Attach the chimes to a bamboo bar.

Wind chimes add appeal of sound to the garden. To make these chimes, use bamboo from your garden, an old fishing pole, or the bamboo that large rugs are rolled around.

WIND BELLS FROM FLOWER POTS

You can make these garden wind bells by rigging up a row of ordinary flower pots. Because they are made of clay, it is possible to leave them out in all weather.

Choose clean pots and test for flaws by tapping. If sound and dry, a pot will ring. The only other materials you need are bone rings (available at department store notion counters), garden twine, and aluminum foil. The aluminum foil tags should be varied in size so they will swing the clappers against the pots at different intervals.

Design by Doris Aller.

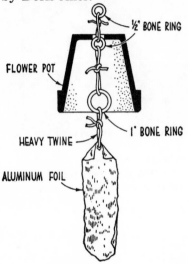

Aluminum foil tags swing clappers against flower pots. Largest pot is 4 inches in diameter, smallest is 1¾ inches. The foil tags also vary in size.

STARFISH IN A HOOP

If you should find a starfish while beachcombing, you can put it to decorative use in your garden or patio.

First step is to dry the specimen. Put it on a flat board, pin the tips of the arms in the shape you want, and leave it in full sun. Turn it over the next day and pin it down. Turn it back the third day to finish drying.

Run a wire through the middle of the starfish and up through the inside of whichever point you think will look best at the top. Continue the wire around a hoop (the cask hoop in the photograph was also found at the beach), and fasten it to a nail, a few inches out from the fence or other background so it will cast a shadow.

Starfish ornament decorates a fence panel. It hangs slightly away from its background so that it swings freely and creates a shadow pattern on fence.

Two wooden bowls separated by 12-inch dowel hang from stout tree limb. Crumbs are spread in lower bowl, upper one keeps off rain. Pine cone is smeared with suet.

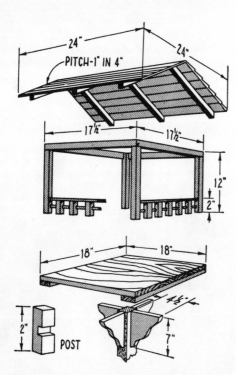

Japanese-style feeding house for birds has wide roof for shelter and to keep feed dry on rainy days. Strictly a job for the craftsman who works for the joy of building things, pieces are prefabricated, then assembled. Use nails, waterproof glue for joinery. Design: R. Kielsmeier.

This unusual feeder tray revolves to give birds shelter when the weather is blustery. Rudders keep it faced into the wind so that the three glass walls can give maximum protection. The feeder is mounted on a flat race bearing. Design is by J. H. Barnes.

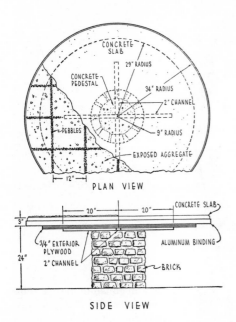

PLAN VIEW

SIDE VIEW

Working plan for construction of table-top feeder shown at right. Concrete slab top is 6 feet in diameter.

The wide overhang of the table top makes it impossible for cats to take the birds by surprise. In order to jump on the feeder, cats must stand back quite a distance, giving birds plenty of time to see them.

TABLE-TOP BIRD FEEDER

When birds dine at this generous table, you can see them easily from the house and terrace. Yet human observers are far enough removed to give a sense of security to shy wild pigeons and other birds that feed at the table several times a day.

The top, 6 feet in diameter, is made of white aggregate exposed in white concrete, bound with a ring of aluminum. The pattern of squares is marked by lines inlaid with blue pebbles.

Supporting the top are crosspieces of 2-inch channel iron set on a concrete pedestal faced with old brick. The pedestal is 18¼ inches high.

Cement was worked into soil under feeder and gravel then raked into it, so spilled seeds don't germinate. Design and construction by Solomone and Hoy.

Left. Swinging feed trough for birds hangs from a tree branch. Two lower perches, made of ⅜-inch dowels, provide a place for birds to rest while feeding.

Simple pattern of aralia leaf is well suited to mosaic. Tiles must be cut to fit the pattern, so simplicity of design is important.

MOSAIC BIRD BATH

The bird bath shown here could be made with almost any pattern you choose. Here, we show exactly how it was done with an aralia leaf pattern.

Technically, making the bird bath is no more difficult than making a simple mosaic hot pad. Cutting the tiles to fit a pattern, however, makes this project far more time consuming. After the cutting, there are approximately 800 separate little sections of tile to place in the frame. From the mosaicists point of view, the job of thinking out the cuts so that all the pieces have a pleasing relationship is one of the great pleasures of the craft. It has much of the appeal of a jig saw puzzle, with the added advantage that you can make up your own puzzle and then enjoy it as a permanent work of art.

Two features of the design make this bird bath a good project for the craftsman who wants to take the next step beyond the simple mosaic project. First, the leaf pattern was kept simple. Second, the color range was purposely very limited. There are only three colors involved—gray-green for the background, and two shades of green (blue-green and bright green) for the leaf itself. The background is light in color, and the two leaf colors are both dark so that they stand out together as one unit against the background. All the blue-green tiles were laid on one side of each leaf segment, while all bright green tiles were laid on the other side.

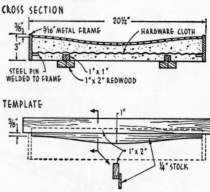

Ring is made of 3/16 by 3-inch hot roll flat bar steel, welded into a circle. It has three small protruding rods inside. Ring was made in a metal shop.

1. Lay iron ring over a sheet of heavy paper. Draw pattern to fit ring. Indicate different color areas on pattern. Remove pattern, save for later steps.

2. Place two ½-by-¾" sticks, with 3 nails in each, inside ring. Mix concrete, trowel into ring. Let nail heads protrude slightly above surface.

3. From hardware cloth, cut a circle that will just fit inside ring. Push it into concrete, hooking it over nail heads. This is reinforcing screen.

4. Add concrete to within 1 inch of top of ring; twirl template (shaped as shown in sketch) in concrete to make shallow depression.

5. To refine bowl shape of bird bath, use metal spatula to go around concrete, smoothing out rings and irregularities left in previous step.

6. To make bird bath easy to mount, attach 1-inch-thick rough redwood or cedar boards with screws to sticks cast into underside in step 2.

7. Cut out tissue paper tracing of the pattern. Lay in the circle and transfer pattern directly to concrete in chalk. Retrace lines with pencil.

8. Cut pieces of tile with nippers. (When cutting, it's a good idea to wear goggles or an eye shield.) Fit pieces in place before final gluing.

9. After tile cement dries, rub in grout. Wipe away excess grout while still wet. Wait two days before filling the bird bath with water.

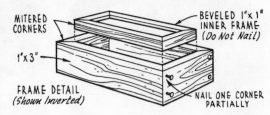

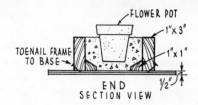

Left. Small potted plants are staged in larger, more stable units. In large unit shown, Haydite creates a lightweight aggregate; in others, beach pebbles produce contrasting texture. Design by John Carmack.

CONCRETE CONTAINERS FOR SMALL POTS

Scores of interesting plants are available in 2-inch pots for the dish garden enthusiast. If they're displayed as potted plants, singly or in collection, the clay pots seem dinky and temporary. But placed within larger, more stable units, the pots are no longer distracting and the plants become all-important. Not only do these containers transform an ordinary plant into a growing gem, but they also keep it in good health by holding moisture around the pot.

To make the containers, use a fairly stiff mix: 3 parts cement, 1 of sand, 2 of pebbles or pumice. Make frame as shown in sketch. To keep wood from absorbing water from mix and to prevent sticking, soak frame in motor oil overnight. Presoak pot in water. Pour frame about half full of mix; twist pot into position, and fill in concrete to top of frame.

Twist pot frequently to prevent sticking and to insure a smooth inner finish. After the concrete firms, brush lightly to expose aggregate. A day later, strip off form and twist out pot. Run water over aggregate surface. After concrete is hard, scrub it with a wire brush.

A container like this is a stage for miniatures. Many variations are possible: integral color in the mix, applied stain, or a terrazzo finish are possibilities.

PLANTERS FROM SLICED ROCKS

The fascinating thing about these planters is that the plants seem to grow out of natural rock. This effect is achieved by slicing apart weathered rocks from the beach or the mountains, taking out a center section, then reassembling the rock.

To make a planter requires six cuts on a diamond saw. If you do not have your own saw, perhaps you can have a rock sliced by a lapidary friend; or take the rock to a lapidary shop.

The first cut levels the base. (If you wish, make an additional cut to level the top.) The next cut takes off a slab that will serve as a base layer for the upper section from which you cut the core. The third cut takes off one side. Cuts 4, 5, and 6 are made around a rectangular core.

As you make the cuts, mark off and place in position the pieces that will stand on the base; the contours of the various pieces may be difficult to match up otherwise.

For an adhesive, use a plastic putty (polyester resin), sold in boat and auto parts shops. The cost, about $5 per quart, includes catalyst—a hardener in a separate container, to be added when you are ready to use the plastic. You can approximate the color of the rock by adding dry poster-color pigment to the plastic putty (before adding the catalyst, so you will have time to mix before the plastic hardens).

CLYDE CHILDRESS

To make these unusual planters, you slice rocks apart and then reassemble them without rectangular core.

Since plastic putty tends to harden on anything it touches, mix it in a paper cup, and use an old knife to stir. After adding the catalyst, apply the plastic putty to the surfaces to be joined, in a layer about ¼ inch thick, and allow it to harden. You can wipe off any plastic from the surface before it hardens.

The diamond saw will give most rocks a pleasantly soft finish. To heighten the color, you can use a water-seal or a slate-dressing preparation, both of which have worn well outdoors.

Planters pictured are by Mrs. Howard Quinn.

Tightening rock for slicing on diamond saw. First two cuts form slab which will become bottom of planter; this cut removes the side. Cut takes 15 to 45 minutes.

Sliced rock is pulled apart to show how cuts are made. In the background, a lantern and another planter have been cut and are ready to be assembled.

These shallow planters were cast in a box holding sand. The sand is molded by hand, then the concrete is troweled to shape. Box defines edge of planter.

PLANTERS OF LIGHTWEIGHT CONCRETE

The strength of these planters comes from their rich mixture. No reinforcing is used. Use a mix of ½-inch Haydite, sand, and cement in a 2-1-4 or 2-3-4 ratio. Concrete should be "stiff," so as not to flow in the mold. For variation, "seed" mold and wet concrete with small aggregate, which will be exposed on the final surface.

To mix the concrete, first mix dry ingredients with a shovel, then add water slowly and mix evenly. Be sure to mix enough; it's not easy to calculate how much you will need, but you can estimate the volume to be filled, and then use half again as much of the dry ingredients. Water compacts the volume. Should you run short, mix up some concrete of equal parts cement and sand for last-minute filling in before the concrete sets up.

When you shovel the concrete into the mold, trowel it quickly into place. The more you trowel concrete, the more likely it is to sag and thus crack—be especially careful if your mold has an inclined surface.

Let concrete cure for a minimum of 48 hours. If you can stand the suspense, it is best to let it cure for two weeks, since concrete gets progressively stronger during this time. In sand casting, just cover the concrete with wet sand. You can also cover it with plastic, burlap, or other materials that will hold the dampness in. If you unveil at the 48-hour stage, be sure not to drop or jar the concrete.

The curved planter shown at right is a logical extension of the principle behind those illustrated

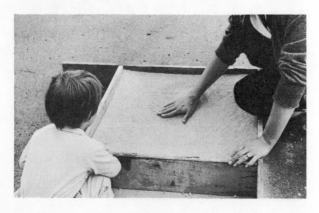

1. Build box to outside dimension. Wipe wood with crankcase oil for easy release. Fill frame with damp sand. Start in center, work sand to shape—evenly all around.

2. Place concrete carefully in mold. Note its stiffness. Cork in bottom is for drain hole in planter. Put concrete in center, then work it out toward the edges with trowel.

Wooden members form base, are structural stiffeners. Boards are set loosely in sand mold. Note cork for drain hole.

Strong "architectural" shape of this planter suggests that it would be appropriate to set off common plants you might not otherwise consider as "show-off" planter subjects. Enlarge the size and depth for larger plants.

here. To make the curved planter, use either of the formulas on page 22. Draw a cross section of the planter on the inside of the form box, so you can control the shape as you form the sand and trowel on the concrete. It is a good idea to repeat the cross section on the wooden members, and then drive nails in them so they will be imbedded in the concrete. This adds rigidity and strength. It's also a good idea to treat the wood with a wood preservative.

Planters pictured on these two pages are by Daniel J. Lieberman.

3. Trowel to shape, avoiding too much working; be careful not to disturb sand. Form should be level for level top corners. Try for a uniform thickness.

4. Cover concrete with damp sand or burlap. Keep damp for 48 hours while curing, then unwrap the wooden form and carefully remove the sand from around concrete.

DARROW M. WATT

Art in the parking area: concrete panel, ornamented by insets of glass, was cast in sand by Virginia Davidson. Technique of sand casting is described on page 31.

DON NORMÁK

Pierced entry panel at end of streetside fence resembles Indian carving. It was cut with jigsaw, chisel, and knife. Edges, grooves are painted. Designer: George Johanson.

Fence and Wall Decoration

Along with the glass wall and the large patio has come the use of fences for privacy. When a fence acts as the wall of an "outdoor room," it can be decorated like a wall. The decoration adds interest to your outdoor room, and it adds to the feeling that the fence is really a room wall. In planning your fence decoration, you can work with color, with pattern, and with the form of the fence itself. You can make decorative tiles or panels a part of the fence, or you can mount them directly on the fence.

In planning fence decoration, you quickly bump into a curious difference between the indoors and the outdoors. A picture, for instance, that is the right size for an indoor wall 12 feet wide under an 8-foot ceiling may look like a postage stamp on a fence 60 feet long under the infinite ceiling of the sky. The viewing distance also makes a difference. Compare the distance you sit from a wall in the house to the distance you sit from a fence in the garden, and you see another reason for making outdoor decoration larger.

Weather makes another difference. For permanence, you must select materials that will take extremes of sun and wind, the soaking of rain, and sharp changes in temperature. However, this doesn't mean the materials must be indestructible. You may want to change after a year or two, as you change pictures and colors on a wall. Remember, too, that weathering can be an advantage. Wood, copper, and brick, for example, become more beautiful as they weather.

Decorative fence panels are made of welded wrought iron rods which have been enameled. Circles are harness rings. By Matt Kahn.

Pink ceramic tiles set in wood frame are decorative background for climbing vine that grows against the house wall. **Below:** Close-up of tiles shown at right. Tiles were made by ceramist Ernie Kim.

FENCE AND WALL DECORATION 25

Above. Mosaic lion mounted on tiles adds color and a touch of whimsy to the garden. Plants will grow up so lion will look out from "jungle." By Virginia Davidson.

Left. In a small entry court, dark house wall is effective background for concrete panel set with projecting bricks enameled in bright colors. Panel by Howard Duell.

Above. Four glazed ceramic tiles mounted in a narrow wood frame make this panel by Mary Erckenbrack.

Left. Carved panel by sculptor Everett Turner was poured in a 2 by 4-foot shallow plywood box. Mixture was plaster of Paris, white cement, perlite (in 7-1-4 ratio). After setting up, mixture was soft enough for easy carving.

A family project, this pebble mosaic facing for a 24-foot bare concrete wall was done by the Richard J. Palmers. Pebbles, gathered on trips, were sorted by color. Mortar was applied in sections on wire mesh foundation held in place with redwood battens and concrete nails. Finished wall was treated with wax to give it richer color.

Above. Smooth river pebbles, carefully selected for shape and color, were used in this mosaic designed and made by Dorothy Puccinelli.

Right. As you approach the garden gate of this Honolulu home, you see this dancing lizard panel. Ceramic panel, by Claude Horan, was done in four sections. It is fastened to the gate by wire brackets. Wall is white-washed rock topped with sisal.

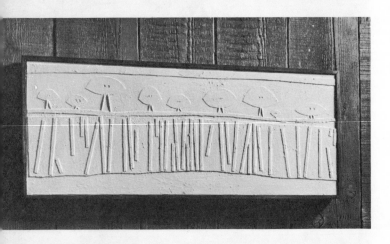

BAS-RELIEFS . . . EASY TO MAKE

The handsome bas-reliefs pictured on this page are surprisingly simple to make. A low relief design is glued and nailed to a plywood backing; the entire panel is coated with exterior primer and paint, then framed. With the addition of a waterproofing agent as described below, the panels can be hung outdoors, preferably in a protected area.

You will need exterior plywood for the background (½-inch thickness for small panels, ¾-inch for larger ones requiring more rigidity); ¼-inch exterior plywood or ⅛-inch tempered hardboard, or both, for the design; waterproof glue, galvanized two-penny finishing nails, a water seal, exterior white primer paint, and an exterior color paint if desired.

Cut the ½ or ¾-inch plywood to size, and draw your design on it in pencil. On the ¼-inch plywood and/or ⅛-inch hardboard, lay out the raised part of the design using thicker pieces where you want higher relief, thinner pieces for lower relief. Cut out the pieces with a scroll saw or a hand saw.

Applying the glue liberally, fix the pieces in position on the backboard, along with other materials (such as string, cardboard, toothpicks, and beads) if you want to use them. To insure a good bond, nail the plywood and hardboard pieces in place. Countersink the nails and fill the holes with putty. If there are too many nails to countersink, coat them with a metal primer instead.

Apply a coat of water seal after the glue has set. Be sure that you saturate all surfaces including the back of the panel, and all the edges of the design. Let it dry for four days, then recoat it. Allow the second coat of water seal to dry for two days. Apply exterior white primer, then a finish color coat if desired.

Jack Millick developed the technique for making these bas-reliefs; the panels on this page are his design.

Top left. "Family portrait" is a conversation piece. The panel is 15 by 23 inches, hangs in protected entryway.

Center left. Simple shapes are repeated to make this long horizontal panel of whimsical heads peering over a fence.

Left. Bas-relief fish are done in ⅛-inch tempered hardboard and string. Panel measures 1½ by 4½ feet.

MOSAICS MADE FROM MILL ENDS

Mosaic panels like these are fun to make. The natural textures and colors of the wood go well together and look their best as decoration for a garden wall or corner.

Wooden odds and ends like these can be found at lumber yards, along the beach, around old houses—wherever your eye catches an abandoned fragment of wood stock that appeals to you.

Saw the pieces to a fairly even thickness (small discrepancies add interest), then arrange them in various patterns. When you are satisfied with a pattern, cut a piece of hardboard big enough to hold it, and cut a frame of 1 by 2-inch stock. Glue and nail the frame, then transfer the pieces to the hardboard, fixing them in place with waterproof glue. You can leave the panels untreated to weather naturally, or coat them with a clear exterior finish.

The panels shown were designed by Doris Aller.

Weathered 4 by 4-inch cubes, some end-on and some exposing chiseled sides, form bold composition.

Panel of wood pieces contrasts subtle color, pattern, and texture variations, resembles a cubist painting. Waterproof glue holds pieces to hardboard backing.

Large mosaic of chiseled mill ends, boards, dowels, new and old, fits nicely into a garden setting.

Cement panel cast in an iron form was designed as part of a plastic garden screen on wood frame. Lengths of rope are dyed black. Designer: F. Alston Swift.

Concrete panels cast in sand by Virginia Davidson. The technique by which panels like these are made is described on the opposite page, pictured on pages 32 and 33.

Concrete cast in a welded iron form and molded in a low relief design forms this handsome panel to dramatize a house wall. Design: F. Alston Swift.

This mosaic to decorate a garden fence is of pebbles, colored glass, and ceramic tile set in cement in wood frame. Design: Virginia Davidson.

ERNEST BRAUN

Sand-cast panel made by Virginia Davidson. Step-by-step photographs on next two pages show technique.

PANELS CAST IN SAND

If you are nostalgic about the fun of playing in a sand pile, this is a project you'll enjoy. You work outdoors, with a basic material that is unusually responsive. It's easy to alter the design if you make a mistake or change your mind. On the following two pages, you'll find step-by-step photographs showing how the panel pictured above was made.

Principal materials you'll need are a 50-pound bag of sand and a 100-pound bag of plaster of Paris. You'll also need 4 pieces of 2-inch by 4-inch lumber for the frame, an assortment of gadgets for making patterns, and a piece of expanded metal an inch smaller all around than the panel.

By experimenting with ordinary kitchen utensils and tools like those in the photograph at right, you will probably come up with some interesting design ideas. Remember that the shapes will be reversed when you cast them: An indented area in the sand will be a raised place on the plaster; patterns on your left, as you look at the mold, will be on your right as you face the finished panel.

Build your mold in a shady, wind-protected spot so the sand will stay wet longer. Before you place the framing boards, pour a bed of sand 2 inches deep and as large as the area of the panel you intend to mold, plus an extra foot on all 4 sides. The panel shown in the photographs is 24 inches by 28 inches. Wet the sand thoroughly

with a hose. Then make a rectangle with the 2 by 4's on edge. Butt the pieces together at each corner, and let two boards extend beyond the others. Square the corners. Add more sand.

When you have filled the surface area of the sand with patterns, mix the plaster of Paris in a large bucket or other container. Measure 2½ gallons of water for a panel 24 by 28 inches. Then gently sprinkle plaster on the surface of the water, letting the water absorb as much as possible, until the plaster forms a slight mound above the water. Let the plaster and water mixture stand for several minutes; then stir it carefully until it is the consistency of light cream. Try to keep any air bubbles out of the plaster as you mix it.

Wash all utensils as soon as you have used them because the plaster may rust metal. When your panel is dry, hang it up by the narrow strip of expanded metal that sticks out from the back. The amount of plaster you've used will make the panel fairly heavy, so be sure to support it well. Choose a sheltered location; plaster of Paris will deteriorate if it is fully exposed to the weather. However, you can make the panel fairly weatherproof if you apply 3 or 4 coats of a clear, water-repellent finish. For a permanent weatherproof panel, substitute a fine concrete mix—with white sand—for plaster. For larger panels, use lightweight aggregate in the mix.

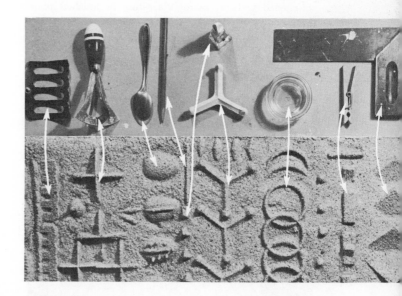

Experimental panel shows patterns made with nine simple objects: spatula, chopper, spoon, pencil, nail polish bottle, ceramic stilt, glass lid, clothespin, right angle.

1. Check top of 2-by-4 frame with a carpenter's level; then pour in sand, using hose to keep it wet. Boards are held together with sand banked against outside of frame.

2. To make the mold, spread sand evenly; use straight-edge to make sure surface is level. The moist sand should fill the wood frame to within 1 inch of the top.

3. Moisten sand with fine water spray to give surface a roughened texture—more interesting in finished panel than smooth surface. Sand should be damp, not soggy.

4. Place heavy paper pattern of the main part of design in center of mold and trace. Hold pattern firmly against surface and press point of pencil well into the sand.

5. Scoop out area inside the traced figure. Start with section that will protrude from panel least (low relief), progress to area that will protrude most (high relief).

6. Press objects in sand to decorate area around main figure. Tablespoon being used above makes leaf-like pattern. Chopper made the crosses at top of the mold.

7. Hollow-centered wood cylinder, pencil, scrap of dowel were used to make patterns in main figure. Small decorations can be about 1 inch deeper than large areas.

8. Pour plaster into the mold with a coffee can. Start with an area that is fairly smooth and let plaster flow into the holes. Be sure the entire area is covered evenly.

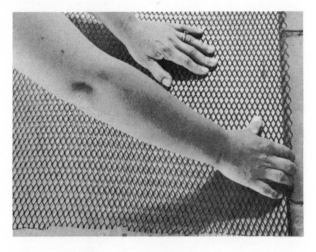

9. Bend top inch of expanded metal over board edge as strip for hanging the panel. Rest of metal will be embedded in plaster and exposed edge will support panel.

10. After plaster hardens 10 minutes, put expanded metal on surface, with bent edge up. Float metal about ¼ inch below surface. If it sinks, remove it and wait a while.

11. Wait 10 minutes more until plaster is hard and warm; then run corner of spatula around edge of mold to remove rough edges and to free plaster from the boards.

12. When plaster fully cools, carefully remove the 2 by 4's. Trim and bevel edges of panel with a sharp knife. Lift the panel gently from mold and hose away sand.

Gaily painted panels of ¼-inch outdoor plywood set in an open frame give a colorful, all-year background to deciduous shrubs and trees. Design: Donn Pierce.

Above. Baffles of 2-by-4 blocks and verticals dress up an entrance. Panel next to doorway is repeated in panel at corner of walk. Design: Armand R. Ramirez.

Below. Horizontal mosaic panel, attached to house siding, has squared edges formed by casting wire-reinforced cement in shallow plywood box. Broken dish and tile fragments make up mosaic. Design: George Johanson.

Above. Cut-out forms of painted plywood decorate this curved screen of expanded metal. Cut-outs are attached to screen with bolts. Design: Eckbo, Dean & Williams.

Below. Decorative look is given to fence panel with plastic inserts of amber, blue, yellow, and rose fitted between the 2-by-2 verticals. Design: Lloyd M. Bond.

Marble mosaic tiles (4 to a panel) are set between translucent plastic panels. Designed by Henry Hill.

White rectangles ornament brown fence in this streetside garden. Retaining walls, designed to preserve existing oak trees, are also painted brown, with a gray-green cap. Design: Roy Rydell.

Hand-made tiles decorate this garden gate. They're pierced, and imprinted and scratched on one side with whimsical designs. Star-like impressions are from eucalyptus seed pods pressed into wet clay. Tiles are held in frame of 2 by 4's by narrow wood stops nailed top and bottom. Gate and fence panels are 1-by-3 tongue and groove with rust stain. Design: Marjorie Wintermute.

Pebble mosaic is a rich accent for a garden, can be a fascinating project for the entire family. Small panels with bold, simple designs work best. Metal strips set off design in above mosaic by Esther Bruton Gilman.

Decorative Paving

Look around your garden. You are almost certain to find at least one spot where you can use a decorative piece of paving to brighten the scene, or where the paving you have could use an accent of some kind to give it interest.

Your paving project may be a simple insert in a bricked patio floor; or it may be a more extensive undertaking such as an inviting garden path of hand-cast stepping stones.

Start with a small job, and if you find you enjoy working with a particular material, go on to a larger one. The pebble mosaic principle, for example, can be applied to a complicated pattern like the one above, or to a simple one like the pebble strip on page 42. If you want to experiment with forming and casting concrete, try a splash

block—you might carve a pattern in it or press pebbles into the block to give it design interest.

There are dozens of ways to add hand-crafted accents to your walks and pavings. Colored beach pebbles, river-washed pebbles, expanded shale, broken bricks are all possibilities to enliven the look of rough concrete. If you have paving blocks or bricks laid in sand, it's easy to remove a few and replace them with squares of a contrasting material.

Stepping stones could be one of your first experiments. Make them by simply digging holes the size and shape you desire and filling them with concrete. You can experiment with any of the various textured surface treatments shown on the pages that follow.

A personal touch in the patio: decorative designs scratched with stick in squares and rectangles of concrete. Design by Robert Royston.

Glazed tile strip creates a rich effect between concrete areas. Glazes are painted on red clay paving tiles, then fired. Tiles by Edith Heath.

Set like pieces of a giant jigsaw puzzle, these concrete slabs form a meandering walk across the lawn area and are an important design element in the garden. Design: Royston, Hanamoto & Mayes.

Two large concrete pads set in gravel parking strip provide firm footing for guests alighting from cars and also add interest to the otherwise plain graveled area. Design: Armand Ramirez.

Small stones pressed into the surface of tinted concrete blocks give contrast and sparkle to paved area of the patio.

PEBBLE BLOCKS

Pebble blocks have a wonderful hand-crafted quality that is completely at home in the garden. There is infinite variety in the kinds and sizes of blocks you can make and in the ways you can lay them; and there is no limit to the size, color, or texture of the stones that make up the pebbly surfaces. For special effects, other materials such as metal, glass, or pottery are good possibilities.

In the photograph below, we have shown a dozen different raw materials that can be used for surfacing blocks, and on the opposite page are some of the textures that result.

There are three ways to make a pebble block. To do it the easiest way, you simply press pebbles (or anything else which will make up the surface) into the concrete which is cast in a mold. Use fairly large stones and be sure to press or pound them far enough down so that the mortar grips them.

The second way is to set the stones on the surface, then work the surface with a steel trowel. Troweling makes the concrete come up to the surface, so the stones will disappear. Then a few hours later—before the concrete is hard but is still a little crumbly—wash the surface with water.

CLYDE CHILDRESS

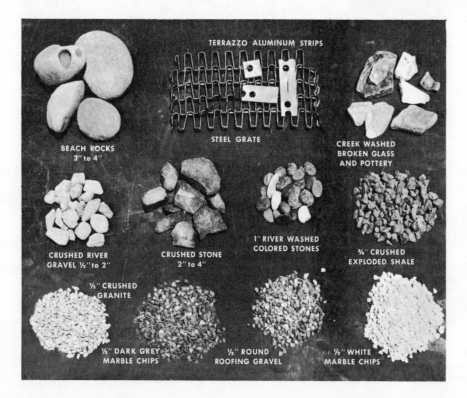

BEACH ROCKS 3" to 4"

TERRAZZO ALUMINUM STRIPS

STEEL GRATE

CREEK WASHED BROKEN GLASS AND POTTERY

CRUSHED RIVER GRAVEL ½" to 2"

CRUSHED STONE 2" to 4"

1" RIVER WASHED COLORED STONES

¾" CRUSHED EXPLODED SHALE

½" CRUSHED GRANITE

½" DARK GREY MARBLE CHIPS

½" ROUND ROOFING GRAVEL

½" WHITE MARBLE CHIPS

Above. Pebble blocks are used here as a transitional line between smooth concrete patio at left and children's play yard at right. Design: Geraldine Scott.

Left. Examples of raw materials that can be used to give different surface textures to blocks. Smooth stones are from beach, glass and pottery bits from creek, steel grating from wrecking yard, marble chips and aluminum strips from building materials supplier, exploded shale and round gravel from a roofing firm.

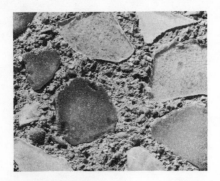

Bits of broken glass with the edges worn smooth, found in creek bed, handset between colored stones.

Steel grate was laid in bottom of mold, green marble chips sprinkled in the spaces, concrete poured on top.

Flat rocks were gathered from beach. The concrete was washed before it dried to get a rougher texture.

Brush away the loose mortar, which washes free, with a burlap sack or a brush. The stones just below the surface will then be clearly exposed.

How fast concrete dries depends upon the temperature, the humidity, the aggregate, and the amount of water in the mix. The first time you make blocks which you plan to wash, it's a good idea to start in the morning. By mid or late afternoon, the blocks should be ready to wash. If you start in the afternoon, the concrete may be too hard the next morning.

The third method is to put whatever you want for a surface texture on the *bottom* of the mold, then pour the concrete on top. This is the trickiest technique. You cannot see the surface once you begin to pour, and it is hard to work the concrete around the edges of each stone.

Each of the three methods described above requires a certain amount of individual experiment and judgment on the part of the block maker himself. However, the following bits of advice should prove helpful no matter which kind of block you are going to make.

When mixing mortar, always add water slowly, for it is easy to get too much. The strongest concrete is made of a fairly dry mix (about like soft modeling clay) which is allowed to dry slowly.

Several days after the blocks have hardened, clean the surfaces with a 10 per cent solution of muriatic acid to remove excess mortar and to bring out the colors of the pebbles. Wear rubber gloves.

Make only small blocks if you don't like to lift a heavy weight. The blocks will vary in weight according to the aggregate you use.

The glass, pottery, or metal-surface blocks have more limited garden use than the pebble-surface ones. Glass or pottery, although bright and colorful in splash blocks under a faucet or drain spout, will fracture if stepped on.

Tan exploded shale, scattered over dark brown concrete, then pressed into place with a wood float.

River-washed stones pressed into block, dentist's tool then used to pick carefully around each stone.

ERNEST BRAUN

Red marble chips sprinkled on white concrete, troweled in, exposed by washing before concrete dried.

Concrete squares have many uses in the garden. Here they form a stepping stone path—less severe than a paved walk—leading from street to entryway.

Concrete rounds, brushed to expose pebble aggregate, repeat curve of patio. Rounds were poured in place in forms of various sizes. Design: Marshall W. Perrow.

Squares of colored concrete are set off against a background of light-colored gravel. A few well-placed succulents, planted in the gravel, add to pattern.

Large rectangular pads of concrete take care of foot traffic and also make an attractive border design between planting area at left and lawn area at right.

LEAF-PATTERN STEPPING STONES

When you add a leaf or flower pattern to a concrete stepping stone, it becomes decorative as well as functional. In fact, you can pick up the mood of the garden in the leaf patterns you choose—a fern pattern for a light delicate touch, a thick philodendron for a tropical effect. In each stone, you can use a combination of plants that grow in the garden, or you might give it the imprint of some plant that grows near it.

The usual method for making stepping stones is to pour the concrete in place, finishing off the tops for a smooth or rough texture. For the leaf pattern, you reverse the process—like making an upside-down cake. You pour the concrete on top of the leaves, then turn the stone over after it sets. Most of the leaf will pull away from the concrete, but some of it will have to dry and rot a little before it comes off.

BLAIR STAPP

For a smooth surface, make stepping stones on piece of plywood. Pour concrete slowly so it doesn't flow under leaves. Use frame if you prefer more rigid shape.

After you pour concrete, tamp it with shovel to settle it and to fill in air spaces. If you don't use frame, mold edges to desired shape while concrete is wet.

WILLIAM APLIN

Leaf patterns lend unusual touch to stepping stones used in this garden path. To place stones, dig out soil and set stones firmly so they won't rock when stepped on.

Let stones dry slowly for a week, until concrete is set. Pull out as much of leaves as you can. The rest will dry and rot out. Wash off the dirt with a garden hose.

Random stone-like shapes are actually earth-colored concrete, set off by areas of flat, smooth stones which were carefully set in place and pressed into mortar.

Broken pieces of red roofing tile are used to decorate paved area. Tile pieces are set in a fan-shaped pattern in concrete, give paving both color and design.

Smooth beach pebbles of various sizes and colors are handset in a narrow band that provides a decorative separation between two areas of smooth pavement.

Pebble block, 12 by 16 inches, was used here in place of six bricks in patio corner. Size of pebble block can be varied to replace more or fewer bricks.

Decorative glazed tiles were hand-painted by Jean Charlot, then kiln-fired and set in a lanai floor of brick. The tiles are white, design is painted in brown.

Inserts of concrete, with fine aggregate to match rest of floor, were cast in sand. Floor was poured around hardened blocks. By Edward M. Brownlee.

Above. A simple way to add decoration to a paving block: six terra-cotta drain tiles were embedded in the concrete to form a pleasing pattern. Design: Osmundson-Staley.

Right. Combination of square and rectangular blocks, some smooth and others of exposed aggregate, give illusion of space at edge of patio. Design by John Catlin.

DECORATIVE PAVING 43

Seahorse panel before doorway is made of flat rocks which were set edgewise in mortar to withstand the traffic in and out of door. Design by Florence Yoch.

PEBBLE MOSAIC

When you make a pebble mosaic, the entire family can join in the project. The smallest members can gather rocks and sort them according to size, color, and texture. Family council can work out the design and colors. The cost of pebble mosaic is negligible, and if your experiment fails to please you, you can chop it out with a mattock and start over. You can practice on small samples—a square under a downspout, a bird bath—before launching your major work of art.

In general, keep your designs very simple. Make strong outlines and mass your colors boldly. You will probably find it helpful to make a preliminary sketch on wrapping paper large enough to cover the entire area. Lay your pebbles over the paper to find out how many you'll need and how they'll look. Plan your design so that you can do a section at a time. From both the mechanical and artistic standpoint, pebble mosaics work out best when used as insets in surfaces of brick or concrete. Fixed borders keep the mosaic tightly in place.

There are two ways of setting the pebbles: they may either be set in mortar or embedded in clay mud. If the clay is properly prepared, it will form almost as permanent a base as the mortar. First provide drainage with from 2 to 6 inches of gravel topped by 1 inch of sand. (If natural drainage is poor, use 6 inches of gravel.) Screen dry clay soil until it is as fine as dust. With the dust, fill in the area where the pebbles are to be inserted to within pebble depth of the surface of the paving. Wet the clay a small section at a time until it is the consistency of dough. Set pebbles on end and close together in the mud. First set them a little high and then press with a plank to embed them evenly and firmly. Sweep off the excess clay. By breaking up the clay soil and then puddling it, you drive out all the air so that when the clay is dry, it is almost impervious to water.

For true permanence, you may want to follow the method of setting pebbles in mortar on a concrete slab. This may be advisable if the panel will receive heavy traffic, as at the front door or gate, or if it is likely to be subjected to erosion due to garden sprinkling or rain runoff.

Mix your mortar with 1 part cement, 2 parts sand, and enough water to give you a mix that doesn't run but spreads easily. You can spread a ½-inch layer of this on top of the concrete slab all at once and level it off with the sides of the board frame in which the slab was poured. Be sure you can get all of your rocks placed in the 1 to 2-hour period you'll have before the mortar sets. If this is not possible, put the mortar in by sections, using a stiffer mix. Smear in a square foot of mortar, fill in the design with rocks, then cut back the dry edges of mortar and smear another section. Your rocks must be wet to give a good bind. You'll have to work more or less freehand since there's no easy way to trace a design on wet mortar.

When the design has been in place 2 to 3 hours, the mortar will have set unless weather is unusually moist. Then tamp dry sawdust down between the rocks with a piece of 2 by 4. The sawdust pushes the stones into the mortar, pushes the mortar down around each stone so it stands out, and levels off the whole thing. After an hour or two, brush off the sawdust with a broom. Try a tentative pass with the broom to be sure stones are firm so you don't budge them. In another hour or so, wash the sawdust off with a brisk fine spray from the garden hose.

Red arrow, set in a background of blue and blue-green tile, points north. Above: after grout was filled in between tiles, surface was cleaned with steel wool.

COMPASS STONE

Choose a prominent location along a walk, or in a patio or entryway, for this bold directional marker. Venetian glass tile in two shades of blue and blue-green forms a background for the bright red arrow. Circle and outline of arrow are brass.

To find the correct angle for the arrow, lay

To make the north indicator, lay a sheet of paper down on the patio or walkway where the square will go. Use compass to find north, then rule north-south line.

down a sheet of paper and rule a north-south line as indicated on a compass. This will give you *magnetic* north; if you want the arrow to point to *true* north, check with your county surveyor to find out what corrections you need to make in order to convert a compass reading of north into true north for your area. Design: Doris Aller.

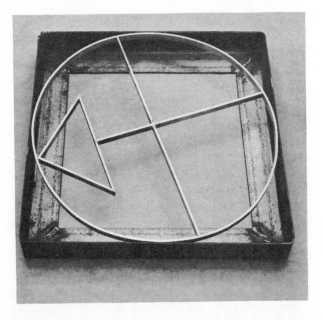

Iron frame that holds the square was welded from angle iron, is 16 by 16 inches, 2 inches deep. Circle and arrow are made from brass strip.

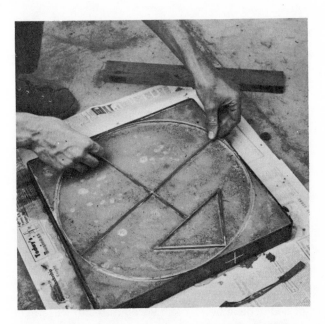

Metal frame was filled with concrete up to about ¼ inch of the top, then it was leveled off smooth with a small trowel before tile was set in place.

Massive cypress root—a perfect piece of natural wood sculpture—occupies an important spot among the rocks near top of a bank overlooking patio. Gray of root, rocks, and soft, gray-foliaged plants creates a luminous effect.

Natural Wood and Stone

A piece of wood or a rock that has been sculptured by nature can, in itself, be a beautiful garden ornament. To the sensitive and discriminate collector, it becomes even more than that. To that person, each piece continues its association with the place from which it came. You can capture the feeling of the High Sierra with a rock, a lodgepole pine, and some granite chips; or recall a rushing stream with a dozen river-washed stones random scattered over a base of pea gravel. A juniper snag or a manzanita root can recall a high windswept crag or a mountain pass. A piece of cedar bleached by salt spray and sun will never lose its touch with the sea; and a log found on a beach at the mouth of a river will suggest a swirling rain-swollen stream.

If you like color, contrast, and variety, wood and stone combine very effectively with plants. It is important to maintain a balance between the size of the piece and the plants with which it is used. Large wood pieces call for large plants. Landscape architects who have been most successful with this type of gardening rarely, if ever, use very small pieces of wood—but long, graceful pieces tie in beautifully with carpeting plants.

The size, shape, and texture of rocks will suggest their arrangement in the garden and the plants to associate with them. Contrasting leaf forms and textures are most effective. There are practical reasons, too, for associating rocks and plants: rocks conserve moisture, hold warmth, and protect plants from sun and wind.

46 NATURAL WOOD AND STONE

Charred redwood sculpture decorates entry. Rice paper plant behind, agapanthus at left, Irish moss ground cover. Design: Lawrence Halprin.

Two pieces of driftwood, a green wine jug, river stones, and glossy green pyracantha form a back-drop for pool made from tank end. Driftwood pieces at right and above by Lana V. Christensen.

NATURAL WOOD AND STONE   47

Graceful sweep of weathered
wood gives a pleasing change
of form and texture in rock
garden. Plants are primroses,
winter aconite, Spring White
heather, and rhododendrons.

CHARLES R. PEARSON

SAMSON B. KNOLL

Driftwood sculpture—exactly as nature carved it—is set
off against light rock surface, darker fence, and delicately
pattern bamboo. Design: Kaye Scott.

RICHARD DAWSON

Imposing 5-foot piece of driftwood is focal point in gravel
courtyard. Pots of sedum, aloe, other succulents add
emphasis. Design: Thomas Church & Associates.

BALDINGER

Conifer root, called "The Thing" by its owners, is displayed dramatically as the main feature in this part of their garden. Drifts of cerastium and lavender form softening mounds in foreground, clematis climbs screen.

NANCY BANNICK

Arrangement of driftwood, planted with succulents, stands out effectively against the light-colored wall next to the entry door. Landscape architect: Richard Tongg.

RICHARD DAWSON

Gray, weather-bleached cypress snag against dark redwood wall in a coastal garden. Succulents grow in cavities in the wood, dwarf cypress behind. Design: Georg Hoy.

SAMSON B. KNOLL

DARROW M. WATT

Native rock found on the owner's foothill property is used to form these steps from redrock path to wood deck. Succulents grow between rocks. Design: Michael Wills.

TATSUO ISHIMOTO

Stones make this adaptation of Japanese lantern. At night the lantern is lit by oil and wick in small glass placed between the two rocks. Design: Kaye Scott.

Smooth pebbles form a stream bed that suggests water although none is there. When sprinkled or washed by rain, the stones look refreshingly cool and clean.

SAMSON B. KNOLL

ROY KRELL

Main and side gardens are divided by pass-through that is flanked on one side by large natural driftwood sculpture, on other by bamboo screen. Design: Kaye Scott.

Smooth rocks of various sizes are a strong design element along the edge of a gravel patio, give pleasing transition between gravel and planting behind. Design: Georg Hoy.

White dolomite simulates a meandering stream through a circular bed of crushed granite and larger stones. Accent plants are succulents, festuca, and azaleas. Design by Mrs. George Kocher.

RICHARD DAWSON

DARROW M. WATT

Curving gravel path, rocks, bulbs, giant bamboo combine to capture feeling of quiet and repose that is so appealing in Japanese gardens. Design: Michael Wills.

WILLIAM APLIN

Contrasting plant forms and leaf textures provide dramatic emphasis against background of massive boulders. Design: Turk Hasselund.

Display panel gives simple background for viewing bonsai. Panel is a 4 by 8-foot sheet of ¾-inch plywood supported by lengths of angle iron anchored in concrete. In many situations, free-standing panels of this type can combine to display plants and to give privacy to a garden area. Plants can be changed from time to time.

Plant Display

Today's architecture in both house and garden creates innumerable situations and backgrounds for plant display—paved areas, capped raised beds, tree wells, screens, and baffles. Container plantings can be the most arresting sights in the garden. A special plant in a special place, an interesting box or tub in just the right setting—these are the little touches that give the garden, terrace, or patio personality and character. Perhaps most of all, containers let you refresh your garden with the seasons.

Azaleas in pots are staged on gravel bed next to house. Bed is edged with brick. Gravel permits good drainage under pots. Design: Florence Yoch, Lucile Council.

Left. Three jade plants in matched containers edge steps leading up to house. These plants grow slowly, retain their shape for many years without excessive pruning. Landscape architect: Richard Beeson.

ROY KRELL

Right. Poured concrete platform at edge of brick patio gets a new treatment every week. Here, *Haworthia margaritifera* is displayed in pot, shell collection below.

WILLIAM APLIN

WILLIAM APLIN

Left. Bonsai collection is displayed on shelf in lath shelter. Interesting variety of containers is the result of patient shopping in old Japanese nurseries and pottery stores.

Pot display bench placed outside a floor-to-ceiling living room window takes the place of a bed of flowers that never looked quite trim. Off the ground, potted plants are free of soil pests and winter dampness. Gravel on ground beneath platform keeps mud from splashing on window when plants are watered, and bed always looks neat.

Pots of succulents add decorative note and provide a touch of color against the white cement steps and retaining wall. Rounded form of these plants is good here.

White marguerites provide color along entry walk. Ten-inch pots slip into holes cut in 1 by 12, are held by pot lip. Display can be changed seasonally. Design: Georg Hoy.

Handsome plant display is gray-green feijoa in brown-stained box made of redwood lath in a vertical lap, nailed to 1 by 12's. Design: Owen Peters, Bettler Baldwin.

Planting bed in *Sunset's* central patio is gravel-paved stage for container plants. Display is changed with the seasons. Bonsai collection above is effective at any time.

Spectacular display of spring color is brought to patio with pots of tulips, azaleas, callas. Succulents are decorative all year round. Design: C. Jacques Hahn.

Right. Dwarf Eustis limequat bears year around in mild-climate areas, dresses up corner of wood deck. White rock mulch in planter adds to decorative effect.

PLANT DISPLAY 55

DARROW M. WATT

MORLEY BAER

Above. Platform, constructed from assorted widths of 1-inch lumber and capped with a 1 by 1-inch strip, has casters so it can be moved to any spot on deck.

Left. Corsican hellebore blooms for several months in the later winter, spring. Chartreuse flowers and pale blue-green foliage are very effective against dark deck.

ROY KRELL

Jade plants in a row of redwood boxes ornament a roof garden. They are easy to care for and always look crisp and green, even under the hottest sun. The simplicity of this planting is especially effective.

Japanese porcelain urns, with patterns of blue and white and a touch of red, add an elegant touch on second-story deck. Junipers grow in wooden buckets set on blocks of wood inside containers to provide drainage. Stands hold urns off deck.

Unusual plant box designed by Georg Hoy is focal point in this low maintenance entry garden.

Redwood stand brings fast color to patio. You simply buy a flowering plant in a gallon can, slip it into place in the stand, and it's ready for display.

Main feature in this entry is the bench built around a Japanese red pine in a tub. Tub rests on ground. Hole at other end of bench contains a small pot of ivy geranium. Design: Kathryn Imlay Stedman.

DARROW M. WATT

Pipe-framed pavilion, designed to shade an area around a tree too young to give shade, was made in shop, assembled in place. Frame is bolted together and canvas laced taut for rigidity. Strips of saran shade cloth give pleasing shade pattern below. Structure can be taken apart and stored. For construction details, see page 60.

Ornamental Sun Shades

On these pages, we've gathered together shade shelters of various types. Some are new and provocative, such as the pavilion pictured above. Others are tried and true. Some are simple to erect, and some are more complex. Each shade idea pictured has a pleasing character of its own. The gay shapes and bright colors suggest carnivals and garden parties. They have a light and airy feeling, restful and refreshing in the summertime garden. Even when their shade is not needed, they are frivolous and fun and will add a decorative note to the garden scene.

For temporary summer shade, parasols anchored in metal umbrella stands bring gay color and inviting shade to any part of the garden. Landscape architect: Georg Hoy.

Above. Tent-like structure uses young shade tree as center pole. Bamboo poles and ropes anchored to tent stakes hold canvas firmly in winds up to 25 miles per hour. Tent is made of triangles of vat-dyed canvas. Design: Osmundson-Staley.

Left. Orange and white alternate in this canvas umbrella suspended from above. Umbrella is 8 feet in diameter. Drawstring around outer edge holds canvas in place over 2 by 1/8-inch welded steel hoop. Shade can be suspended from a tree, a braced support, or a rope between high points.

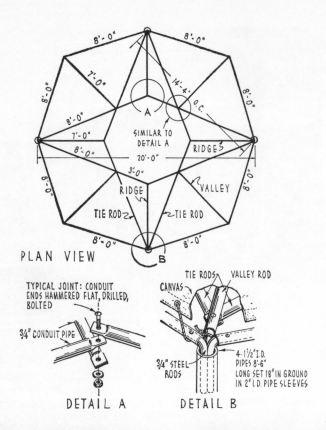

PLAN VIEW

Labels in plan view: 8'-0", 8'-0", 7'-0", 14'-4" O.C., 8'-0", 8'-0", 8'-0", SIMILAR TO DETAIL A, A, 7'-0", RIDGE, 8'-0", 8'-0", 20'-0", 3'-0", RIDGE, VALLEY, TIE ROD, TIE ROD, 8'-0", 8'-0", B

TYPICAL JOINT: CONDUIT ENDS HAMMERED FLAT, DRILLED, BOLTED

3/4" CONDUIT PIPE

DETAIL A

TIE RODS   VALLEY ROD
CANVAS
3/4" STEEL RODS
4-1½" I.D. PIPES 8'-6" LONG SET 18" IN GROUND IN 2" I.D. PIPE SLEEVES

DETAIL B

ERNEST BRAUN

Demountable frame is electrical conduit on four pipe uprights. Conduit ends are flattened, drilled for bolt holes, and bolted, or bolted over ½-inch rods to fit into pipe uprights. Structure has 7-foot hole in center for tree, no center posts, spans 20 feet.

Left. Enormous (18-foot) hanging umbrella with translucent plastic cover diffuses sunlight into soft glow, reflects night lamplight. Design: Royston, Hanamoto, and Mayes.

Sketch below shows bicycle-wheel structure, a laminated wood tension ring. The steel wires link ring to hub, form conical shape for industrial-weight vinyl sheet.

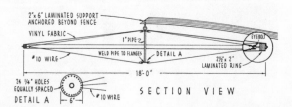

2"x 6" LAMINATED SUPPORT ANCHORED BEYOND FENCE
VINYL FABRIC
1" PIPE
#10 WIRE
WELD PIPE TO FLANGES   DETAIL A
EYEBOLT
2½"x 2" LAMINATED RING
18'-0"
24 ¼" HOLES EQUALLY SPACED
6"
#10 WIRE
DETAIL A
SECTION VIEW

Laced canvas forms these two unusual shelters. Pipe frame is used for the rounded tepee; pipe ring and 4 pipe legs support the canvas circle.

Just a square of fabric and a simple system of support can give you color and shade for a corner of the garden.

KEN MOLINO

Tent of redwood snow fencing, hung like fabric, rises 18 feet on 2-inch (inside diameter) pipe posts, with pipe braces at ends. Its shade varies with the angle of slope. Design: Royston, Hanamoto, and Mayes.

ROBERT C. CLEVELAND

MORLEY BAER

Two ideas for supporting Japanese parasol or garden umbrella. Soy tub at left has two pipes to support parasol either straight or at angle. Right: Umbrella is centered in redwood tub before soil and plants are added.

ORNAMENTAL SUN SHADES 61

Water splashing from bowl to rocks brings sound to this garden pool. Design: Courtland Paul.

Simplicity is the keynote in this pool design. Gravel, boulders, and choice plant material—used with restraint and placed with care—combine effectively to form a pleasant natural setting for small free-form pool.

Water as Decoration

The enchanting quality of water—quiet and reflecting, or dancing and sparkling—can bring beauty into a garden. A simple, shallow reflecting pool is enough to create a "water picture." The reflections of sky and clouds, or a piece of garden sculpture, or an arching branch of a nearby tree add to the picture.

Water adds luster to many materials—tile, brick, wood, concrete, stone, plants—when they become wet. Anyone who has collected gem-like wet pebbles and seen them change to dull dry rocks understands this kind of water use. A garden pool is an ideal showcase for a collection of rocks or shells that show their best colors when they are in water. The bottom of a shallow pool is a good place to display handsome mosaics.

To the plant collector and gardener, a garden pool opens up a whole new world. Long used to the notion that he should try to give plants good drainage, he enters a form of gardening in which the object is to drown the plants. Most water plants add new forms and textures to a garden, especially the hardy and tropical water lilies, with their big leaves and striking flowers.

To give water another element of interest, you can add motion—put fish in the pool, or move the water itself. A slight breeze will ripple the surface of a pool, but a waterfall or fountain gives it real action.

With fountains and waterfalls, you get another interesting feature—the sound of water dripping or splashing down. It's a cooling sound on a hot summer day, and if the pool is placed on the windward side of a patio, the water will actually cool the air flowing over the sitting area. If you can hear the water, you don't have to see a pool to enjoy it. Remember camping by a lively brook or stream, or sleeping where you could hear the sound of the surf?

Look at the photographs on these pages and you'll see that there is no set design pattern for a garden pool. You can start out small and alter the pool as your needs change, or you can start right out with a pool completely equipped with drain, fountain, and circulating pump. Just about anything that holds water can be used for a pool (but don't put fish in a tub made of galvanized metal —it may poison them). Good miniature pools include wood tubs or half barrels, glass fiber pools, old laundry tubs, or surplus plastic bowls. A good-sized pool should have some sort of overflow drain for excess rain water.

MORLEY BAER

Small portable pools challenge the imagination. If you rummage through a second-hand store or storage room, you will usually turn up good candidates for a small pool. This one is a war surplus glass lens.

FRANCES M. CALLAHAN

Above. Discarded laundry tub becomes a miniature garden pool. Owners sank tub along edge of patio slab, planted baby's tears to hide edges. Pool has goldfish, snails, pigmy water lilies. Glass "bubble" floats on surface.

ERNEST BRAUN

Left. Pool made of lightweight aggregate decorates the end of a long garden bench. Bowl-shaped barbecue was used as mold. Glass floats, driftwood add decorative touch.

WATER AS DECORATION 63

ERNEST BRAUN

1. Excavate for pool and lay in drain and intake pipes. The ground under pool should be well packed to form a good base for the concrete.

2. Metal or wood forms around the top give a neat edge to guide your work as you finish the concrete, but form is not an essential for building this pool.

3. Concrete is gradually poured into the depression and then troweled to the desired shape. Wire mesh set into the concrete gives strength.

HOW TO CONSTRUCT A CONCRETE POOL

One of the easiest ways to make a garden pool is to scoop out a depression in the ground and then pour concrete into it, as shown in the photographs. The ground underneath should be well packed to form a base for the concrete. Better provide a cushion of tamped sand or 3 or 4 inches of tamped sand and gravel if the soil freezes and heaves in winter or if it is adobe. Use a fairly stiff mixture of 1 part cement, 2 parts sand, and 3 parts pebbles or gravel. Pour sides and bottom at the same time.

Generally speaking, the sides and bottom of a garden pool made of concrete should be between 4 and 6 inches thick, with wire mesh reinforcing running through about the middle.

The plumbing for filling and draining a pool doesn't have to be fancy. In fact, you can fill a good-sized pool with the garden hose and drain it the same way. But intake valves and drains are very convenient and less trouble. Drains can be connected to sewer lines or to a dry well or sump filled with gravel.

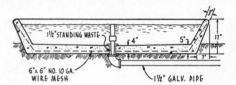

The sketch above gives you the plan for a raised pool that requires forms on two sides. If you move the drain out to the side, you could build this pool over an existing concrete patio without tearing up anything or doing any excavating.

Setting the forms at the angle shown is tricky if the pool is round. The sketch below shows you a way of making the form with 1 by 6-inch

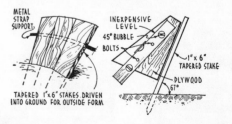

stakes, held together with a metal strap. The device above can be used as a guide so you can get the stakes in at just the right angle.

The revolving template below is one way to get an even thickness on the inside of the pool. You trowel the concrete, then revolve the template to smooth the wall and to remove surplus.

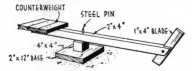

After you finish and surface the pool (place the rocks or mosaic tile before the concrete sets up), let it stand for about 3 days. Cover the concrete with wet sacks so it doesn't dry too fast. Keep sacks moist.

Water in a new pool is very alkaline and hence toxic to fish. There are effective new ways to speed up the leaching out of the alkali in the concrete, but this old method is still the safest: Fill and drain the pool every day for about 3 days; fill again and let the water stand for about a week; then drain and refill and wait for 24 hours for the chlorine to dissipate. You can skip this last step if you use well water.

PUMP INSTALLATION

A circulating pump is the thing to have if you want a fountain or waterfall in a garden pool. There are many pump and motor combinations obtainable—enough to take care of any usual

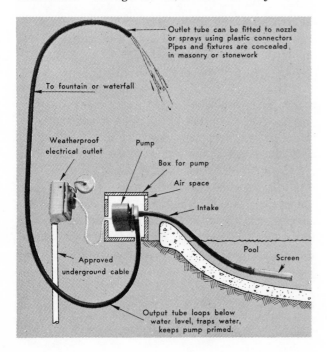

4. Rocks or other decorative objects can be pushed into the concrete before it sets up. If such decoration is not added, smooth or finish off surface of concrete.

5. Let concrete dry slowly (cover with wet sacks and keep them moist during the curing period). Then fill pool. Follow instructions at left before adding fish.

garden pool requirements. They vary in power, capacity, and price. You can buy pumps for installation above or below the water level of the pool. Some types sit right in the water and need only to be grounded and plugged into an electrical outlet. The manufacturers of small pumps will help you plan your installations and advise you on the pump size you need.

Get a pump that delivers a little more water than you need. You can always control the flow of water by a valve or by simply pinching the hose or tube with a clamp. Be sure to use fittings of the same diameter as those on the pump. That is, if the output and intake fittings are $\frac{1}{4}$ inch, use $\frac{1}{4}$-inch fittings to connect pump and fountain. You don't get a faster flow by going to an output pipe or tube of smaller diameter. You just increase the amount of friction and lower the

Above. Fountain in circular entry pool splashes over red rocks in center by overflow drain. Inside of pool is covered with aluminum paint. Design: Lawrence Halprin.

Above left. Fern-framed log in raised bed is setting for this "pool"—a 12-inch pottery bowl filled by ⅛-inch hose hidden in overhanging Japanese maple.

efficiency of the pump. To get the jet effect, pinch the tube close to its output end.

For best performance a circulating pump should have a flooded intake. The illustration on page 65 shows a typical pump installation. You'll notice that the pump is above the level of the water, but that the output pipe or tube loops down from the pump below the water level before it swings up to the fountain. This loop traps water and keeps the pump flooded. You can do the same thing with the intake pipe or tube, looping it below the water level before running it into the pump. Of course, if the pump is set below the level of the water, it's automatically flooded and primed.

If the pump isn't flooded, you'll have to prime it before it will start. Force water from the garden hose up the intake pipe until it squirts from the output pipe or tube. Then remove the garden hose and turn on the pump. Remember that you may have to prime a new pump the first time even if it's set in a flooded position.

Running the electrical cord from the pump to a weatherproof outlet can be tricky business. Call in an electrician if you are in doubt. He knows the regulations that govern electrical installations. If you do the job yourself, be *sure* to get

Left. Copper tubing is curved and angled into whimsical fountain that sends jets of water in crisscross pattern. Design: Eckbo, Dean & Williams.

a permit from your local building inspector if you are making this a permanent installation tied directly into your electric lines and controlled with a switch.

PLANTS AND FISH

When you start to stock your garden pool with plants and fish, you're in for a real treat. The number of water and bog plants displayed in water gardens seems to be endless: water lilies with white, yellow, peach, pink, red, blue, and purple flowers (hardy and tropical varieties need a pool 18 inches to 2 feet deep); water poppies; lotus; floating plants of all kinds; and bog plants that grow in only a few inches of water.

In the photographs at right, we show you a representative group of water plants and 7 varieties of goldfish for an outdoor pool. Commercial water gardens ship fish and water plants; check their catalogs for lists of plants, fish, and desirable scavengers.

Of course, a dish or bowl pool is not the ideal environment for fish. Because of the size of the container, the water heats and cools much too rapidly for most fish. In fact, in a sunny spot, fish may just escape being parboiled. It's a good idea to skip the fish and just use such things as floats, flowers, rocks, or wood for decoration in small portable pools.

Since mosquitos can breed in a small tin can of water, a garden pool can become a major hatchery for these pests. However, mosquito fish (*Gambusa affinis*) thrive on mosquito larvae. About 1 to 1½ inches long, these fish are greenish on top and silvery on the sides and bottom. They will wiggle through very shallow water for the larvae and seem to tolerate pool conditions that would quickly kill many other types of fish.

CLEANING THE POOL

Most garden pools need a real honest-to-goodness cleaning and revamping about every two or three years. By then most water plants need thinning or dividing and replanting. Decayed

Right. Bog plants grow in pots or boxes set on stones or ledges in pool. There should be about an inch of water over crowns of plants. Gravel mulch holds soil in place.

BLACK MOOR or (Veiltail Moor)

COMMON

VEILTAIL

FANTAIL

SHUBUNKIN

CALICO

COMET

CLYDE CHILDRESS

When you begin to stock your garden pool with fish, you have many choices. Here are seven varieties of goldfish. Check commercial catalogs for other fish and plant life.

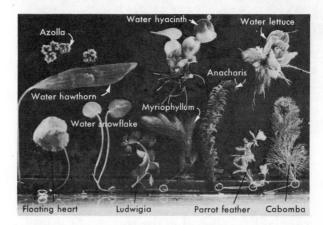

Azolla

Water hyacinth

Water lettuce

Water hawthorn

Anacharis

Water snowflake

Myriophyllum

Floating heart

Ludwigia

Parrot feather

Cabomba

Collection of water plants that float or grow under water. They provide shade, oxygen for fish, and help pool to reach a balance that will keep down growth of algae.

Pickerel plant

Cattail

Dwarf papyrus

Water arum

Water plantain

Horsetail

Umbrella plant

Iris versicolor

ART HUPY

Water spray jet, home-assembled from pipe fittings and a pipe-to-hose adapter, is set among moss-covered lava rocks in cool garden corner. Design: John Carmack.

Rocks set around pool hide concrete edges, give pool a natural look. In one section, the turf curves over pool sides to meet the water. Design: Noble Hoggson.

material has collected in the bottom of the pool, forming a messy crust, and algae has accumulated on the sunny sides of the pool. A dirty, plant-choked pool is not pleasant to look at, nor is it a healthy environment for fish and other animal life.

If your garden pool is ready for a good scrubbing, here are a few helpful tips to make the job easier:

Removing the fish. Fill a large tub or bucket with water from the pool and set it to one side. Don't use fresh tap water for the fish unless you let it sit for about 24 hours before you put the fish in it.

If the pool has a built-in drain, scoop up all the fish and snails and place them in the tub or bucket of pool water. Then open the drain. If the pool is fairly large, put a fine mesh screen or strainer over the drain and lower the water level until you can catch the fish easily.

If there is no drain and some spot close by is lower than the pool, use a siphon to remove the water. A garden hose works wells. Fill the hose

with water, holding the loose end upright at the same height as the faucet. Plug up that end with your thumb and disconnect the other end from the faucet. Place a fine mesh screen over this end of the hose and plunge it into the pool. When you lay the opposite end lower than the pool, the siphon action should start. You can leave the fish in the pool until almost all the water is gone. Then move them into the tub or bucket. Place the container of fish in a cool spot.

Cleaning the pool. Remove all plant containers from the pool. Scrub the grime and algae off the bottom and sides of the pool with a stiff brush and water—you can use soap if you make sure to rinse out the pool two or three times afterward. You stand a better chance of rinsing out all the soap if the pool has a built-in drain than if you have to rely on a siphon or bailing bucket.

Check for cracks and leaks. Clean out cracks and fill and cover with a ribbon of asbestos plastic cement. (Don't confuse the term "plastic cement" with one of the glue products.) If the

Galvanized sheet metal, left over from house, forms half-moon pool 8 inches high, 18 inches wide. Metal is painted but is still harmful to fish. Design: Kent McCoy.

Splashing fountain creates a cool atmosphere in this entry garden. Wild strawberry forms a lush ground cover around the pool. Design: Lawrence Halprin.

pool bottom or sides tend to seep, mix waterproof plastic cement with water until it is the consistency of paint, then brush it on. If you have a tile-lined pool, you may have to replace a tile or pack more mortar into the joints. After repairing material is thoroughly dry, be sure to wash out the pool about three times before you refill it. Some of the soluble substances in cement are injurious to fish.

Taking care of the plants. Water lilies should be divided and replanted in fresh soil about every two years. Discard the old woody portions. Plan on only one lily plant for every 8 square feet of pool area. A white pine box 20 inches square and 10 to 12 inches deep makes a satisfactory container and will last many years under water. Don't use redwood as it discolors the water. Fill the box three-fourths full with a mixture of 3 parts heavy soil and 1 part rotted manure. Some gardeners prefer to pack 2 inches of manure in the bottom of the box, adding the soil over it to prevent any possibility that the manure might foul the water.

Set the water lily crowns so they are about level with the soil. Then spread a 2-inch layer of sand and gravel over the soil and around the plant. This keeps the fish from swishing up clouds of mud as they swim under the plants.

Trim back water grasses and separate the ones that are overcrowded.

Refilling the pool. Replace the plant material and refill the pool. Wait about a day before you add the fish. Prop up the boxes of water lilies so the tops are about 8 to 10 inches from the water's surface.

Fish don't like a sudden temperature change, so many pool owners float the tub or bucket containing the fish in the pool for a few hours until the water temperatures are about the same. (You can buy a commercial product that helps tone up and age the pool water.) Then they tilt one end of the tub down and let the fish swim out into the pool. In any case, don't throw the fish into the pool; let them swim out of the container into the fresh water.

ERNEST BRAUN

Assorted pebbles, as varied as those in a river-made cove, are embedded in mortar. Design: Lawrence Halprin.

DECORATIVE PEBBLE POOL

A decorative pattern not only brightens a pool but shows the stones and shells at their best, for the water intensifies their colors.

If you prefer, you can work out your design first, as the professional does. But if children are involved in the project, you may wish to assemble your pebbles and shells and then just let the design develop as you go along.

If you have only a few pebbles and shells to place, the simplest way to embed them is to push them into the wet concrete soon after it is poured, before it sets. After the shells and rocks are in place, let the concrete harden for about 3 or 4 hours. Then carefully wash the concrete off the pebbles and shells, using a gentle stream of water from the garden hose and a soft wire brush or a broom.

If you plan to decorate the entire bottom and sides of the pool, or if you plan to use a large number of objects in your pool "mosaic," you won't be able to finish the design before the concrete sets. Then the best method is to set them in a layer of mortar spread over the cured concrete surface. The concrete should be rough so there will be a good bond with the mortar. If you use this method, you can work along as you please, doing a small section of the pool at a time.

First, wet down the concrete so it won't draw water from the mortar and cause it to dry too quickly. Then spread a 1-inch-thick layer of mortar in a patch about a foot square. Dip the pebbles and shells in water (this not only cleans them but also wets them so they won't absorb water from the mortar). Then set them in the mortar. When you've finished a foot-square area, spread another patch of mortar, and continue placing the stones and shells. Each day after you have set as many pieces as you want, discard any excess mortar before it sets. Start with a fresh batch the next day. Mix only as much at one time as you think you'll need.

You'll have to experiment until you get just the right mortar consistency. This is particularly important when you're decorating the sides of the pool. If the mix is too wet, it may slide into the bottom of the pool; if it's too dry, the decorative pieces may fall out.

When the mortar has set, use a brush to clean off the pebbles and shells and to smooth off any rough spots in the mortar.

The examples shown here utilize only pebbles and shells, but you can also use such materials as small tiles or pieces of colored glass, china, or pottery. To save time when you're working, it's a good idea to separate the pieces in advance by size and color.

Close-up view shows textures of pieces used in decorative pattern of a pool designed by Douglas Baylis.

Three-tiered fountain cast in plywood forms. Lower pool is cast around post; upper one around pipe for water from a recirculating pump. Design by Charles B. Shaw.

THREE-TIERED CONCRETE POOL

Here is a project for the man with advanced woodworking skill—and confidence. Plywood forms (½-inch) were used so the corners would be sharp. They are shown in the sketch below.

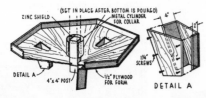

Legs were the difficult part of fitting the form together, and the forms needed considerable shoring-up to support the concrete. The sketch at right shows the bottom pool of the three.

The formula was 4 parts aggregate, 2 coarse river sand, 2 cement, and 1 fire clay. Aggregate was 2 parts of ⅜-inch Haydite to 1 part fine aggregate. The finish coat was 1-1 sand and cement, to assure its being waterproof. About ¼ pound of color was added to the mix.

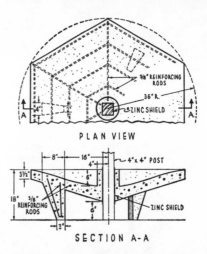

PLAN VIEW

SECTION A-A

Zinc flashing, applied with mastic, protects the wooden post against deterioration. The ¾-inch galvanized pipe supports and drains for the other pools were cast right in the concrete. Water is pumped to the top of the upper pipe; it falls from pool to pool and drains through a tube in the planting bed to the pump.

WOK-FORMED BOWLS

Here is a worthwhile method if your landscape scheme calls for repeating a bowl several times. These bowls have such a finished look that they can also be used in many indoor situations. The compression mold is made of two Chinese *woks*, 32 and 28 inches in diameter, with welded brackets to hold them in place. The woks can be used afterward. The formula is 1½ buckets (10-quart size) cement, 1½ buckets lightweight sand (resembles Haydite), ½ bucket Haydite, and about 8 quarts of water.

After the bowl is removed from the wok mold, wrap it in cloth. Keep it damp and in shade for a week so the concrete will cure.

Precision molded concrete bowl holds water hyacinths. Bowl was cast in Chinese *wok*. Design: Mrs. Clark H. Gates.

DARROW M. WATT

1. Form chicken wire mesh for reinforcing. Both woks are greased so concrete won't stick.

2. After pouring, trowel concrete roughly into shape. Work mesh into the middle of the concrete.

3. Attach brackets to position woks for even thickness of bowl. Place stones in center for weight.

4. Close-up view of brackets that hold woks in position. They're welded, are easily tightened.

5. Finish edge with knife. Next day, remove stone weight and top wok; turn over lower wok, holding bowl.

6. Bottom wok comes off with mallet taps. Wrap bowl in cloth. Keep damp and in shade for a week.

High relief of this fountain forms shallow pools to catch and direct water that bubbles from a plastic hose cast in block. A hose connection, out of sight behind the fountain, hooks to a faucet or pump line.

Above left. Cover bottom of mold with sand. Bend ¼-inch rod for projections and wire; then bend metal mesh over them. **Above right.** Pour 1 inch of concrete. Position hose and cover with mesh; then pour 3 inches.

Above left. Cover bottom with inflated balloons. Work the concrete under, around sides, almost covering balloons. Let cure. **Above right.** Remove parts not wanted; trim with wood rasp. Repair with concrete and slurry.

A SCULPTURED WATERFALL

This fountain first took shape on its back as a slab with a three-dimensional grille on top. It was cast of vermiculite concrete (in a 3-2-2 vermiculite-sand-cement ratio), reinforced with metal mesh and ¼-inch rod. Water-filled balloons (the heavy kind) formed the mold for the grille. (When the concrete sets, you empty balloons and remove them.) The fountain took 3 cubic feet of vermiculite, 1½ of cement, and 1½ of sand, plus ¼ of fireclay.

Cast a plastic hose in the slab with its coupling protruding at the bottom of the back and a loose end near the topmost catch basin. Trim the top so it will be unobtrusive. The coupling connects the hose to a garden hose water source or to a recirculating pump line.

You can work the concrete easily after it sets but before it cures. Chip away grille elements to fit your design. You may have to build up some of the basins and fill in depressions with the concrete mix with fireclay added (use ⅛ as much fireclay as you do cement). After concrete has cured, set the fountain up and try the water flow. You can alter it with a wood rasp and build it up with the concrete mix, over a slurry of cement and water brushed on to make it adhere. Smooth with a wire brush.

Design: Clyde Childress.

Graceful circular fountain designed by Virginia Davidson. Bowl of fountain is embellished with pieces of mosaic glass which provide small accents of color.

RAISED CIRCULAR FOUNTAIN

Casting this graceful raised fountain for the patio or garden is a good weekend project for the family. Pick a fairly sheltered spot so the wind won't blow the spouting water out of the fountain. (Also consider seasonal variations in weather or garden conditions, and night lighting possibilities.) Once you have picked your location, be sure there is enough clearance to work on all sides.

Here's what you will need to build a fountain approximately 4 feet in diameter:

```
100 lbs. cement
  2 tons builder's sand
150 lbs. ¼'' pea gravel
 10 feet ⅜'' copper pipe
 10 feet ½'' copper pipe
       (depends on fountain-to-pump distance)
  1 watertight 5-gal. container to hold pump
  1 submersible 60-cycle pump
 40 feet ¼'' steel rods
  1 pc. 1 by 4'' lumber, 3 feet long
  1 pc. ¾'' plywood, 7 by 10''
  2 mending plates
  2 orange juice cans with top and bottom removed
```

You can lay out the fountain by describing a circle with a piece of chalk on one end of a string equal to the radius.

Your next step is to set the pipes in the ground and pour part of the footing. The footing is a block of concrete (a standard mix, or ready-mix) about 2 feet square. It prevents the fountain from tipping. Dig the footing hole about 14 inches deep. At the same time dig a trench for the pipes from the footing hole to the site you have picked for the pump.

Now, bend the copper pipes to a 90° angle so that the tops of the pipes will project about 3 inches above the height of the completed fountain. Set the pipes in the trench, and check them with a spirit level to see that they are perpendicular to the ground on all sides. Mix enough concrete to fill about 8 inches of the footing hole. Allow it to harden overnight so that the pipes will present a solid pivot for the template.

While the concrete is setting, you can make your template and cut the reinforcing rods. The same template is used for both the inner and outer shape of the fountain—the lower part for the base, the upper part for the bowl. You can make a more elaborate fountain with a curved template, but

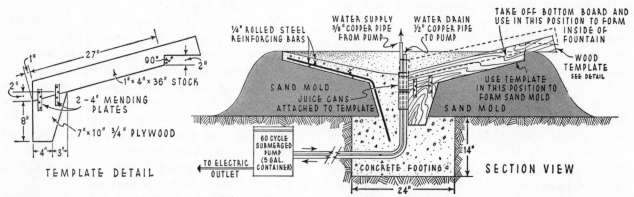

Template made from scrap lumber.　　**Cross-section** of fountain shows details of composition and construction.

VIRGINIA DAVIDSON

1. Sketch position of fountain on patio. Partly constructed template is useful for checking radius. **2.** Cut through patio surface to prepare ground for footing.

3. Cut reinforcing rods to correct lengths. Bend the two long rods into circles. **4.** Nail two orange juice cans to template to act as collar to pivot on center pipes.

remember that once you shape the mold, you must be able to lift the template off the pivot without disturbing the sand.

Next, cut the reinforcing rods. You will need eight 3-foot sections, which you bend to match the angle of the template. These rods will radiate like spokes from the edge of the bowl and extend down into the footing to support the structure. Cut 2 more rods for circles—one 2 or 3 inches smaller than the outside of the fountain, the other with about ⅓ the diameter.

The second day, pour the remaining 6 inches of the footing, bringing it to ground level. Make this portion of the mix dry enough to support the weight of the sand, but soft enough to receive the reinforcing rods at a later stage.

Now build your mold by piling wet sand under the template as you swing it on the copper pipe pivot. Keep sand wet, and compact it with your hands as you go.

Mix the concrete as follows: 1 part cement, 1 part gravel, 1 part sand, and about 1 gallon of water to every 100 pounds of aggregate.

Remove the template and pour the concrete into the footing hole. Trowel it from the center toward the edge in one direction only, so as not

to disturb the sand. Cover the entire mold with a 1-inch layer of concrete, and trowel it smooth.

Place the reinforcing rods on the concrete, pressing the bent spokes well into the footing. Tie each point with light wire where the circles and spokes intersect. Be sure the reinforcing grill lies flat so it will be completely imbedded in the concrete when you pour your final layer.

Pour another 1-inch layer over the grill. Remove the bottom section from your template, and use the top section to smooth the bowl. Radiating, fan-like ridges can be made by jogging the template at equal intervals. Trim the edges before the concrete sets.

Keep the fountain damp during the next 2 days while the concrete sets.

Finally, fit the feed pipe with an adapter that sends up 3 sprays of water to different heights. The adapter is made to different heights. The adapter is made by drilling a threaded pipe cap to receive three 3/16-inch copper pipes, which are welded in place and fitted with nozzles.

Cut the half-inch return pipe to the level of the water in the fountain, and cover it with a copper screen to keep dirt out of the pump, which is set underground.

5. Set pipes; check with level to be sure they are perpendicular. **6.** Pile sand under template and form mold. When template sweep touches sand evenly, you can pour.

7. Press rods into 1-inch layer of concrete; bend spoke sections down into footing. **8.** Pour top layer; then use template, with footing removed, to level surface.

Experiment to see which plants take the light best. This striking plant is an azara—not especially distinguished by day but beautiful when lighted.

Twinkling candles in hurricane lamps are placed on fence posts to shine a cheerful welcome and mark long drive that leads to house.

Decorating with Light

A garden decorated with the magic of light is a beautiful and dramatic sight. Under the bright light of day, all the garden is revealed—the flowers and the weeds, the planting beds and the compost pile, the finished and the unfinished. With night lighting, you have more control of garden effects. You can blot out disagreeable backgrounds or plants out of bloom by simply leaving them dark. You can light one particular tree or group of plants at the height of its beauty; you can even let shadows of trees, branches, and structural objects add their design qualities to your garden.

You can learn a lot about light from nature. Moonlight won't move the needle on a photographer's light meter, but still, it touches a scene with soft highlights and provides enough light to see your way, enough for conversation, enough to transform the most drab objects into beautiful ones. You can achieve the effects of moonlight with well-diffused garden lighting. You can also work toward some of the dramatic effects of nature, like sunlight shimmering on a flowering tree.

You may want to experiment with colored light. Green and blue lights accent foliage color. Yellow and red lights give warm accents.

Before you can work magic with light, you must first learn something of the magician's trade. There are a few rules, but experience is the best teacher. Spend an evening in your garden with some extension cord and a few reflector lights. In an hour or so, you can try half a dozen of the effects pictured in this chapter and see for your-

FIVE WAYS TO LIGHT AN ARALIA

There are five basic effects you can get when you shine a light on a plant. All garden lighting is a combination of these effects. To illustrate them in their simplest form, we have taken one dramatic plant—the aralia—and lighted it to show each of the five ways to light a plant. Look at the plants in your garden and decide which kind of lighting suits them best. When you understand the range of effects that are possible, you can give more direction to your experimenting. First step is to study the form of the plant—and its setting in the garden—to see what it calls for.

CLYDE CHILDRESS

A floodlight is the nearest to daylight. It shows the plant much as you see it in the sun, but with dark background.

Spotlighting is selective floodlighting —like sunlight through a funnel. Here it dramatizes a cluster of leaves.

self how they work in your own situation.

With one plant, you can learn five basic ways to use a direct light—as shown above and below.

You also can experiment with reflected light, which has a wonderful soft quality quite different from direct light. Try bouncing it off a light-colored wall or ceiling to create a large diffused light source. You can hide the light in a cove or with a baffle.

Light not only illuminates objects beautifully, but it also can be a thing of beauty itself. A translucent panel lighted from behind is a glowing decorative screen. The dancing flame of a candle or torch is exciting, although it may illuminate nothing. Japanese lanterns shed little light, but they give a party mood.

The human eye can accommodate only a limited range of light with comfort. This is one reason why it is a good idea to conceal or diffuse all harsh direct light sources. It is not the intensity of the light itself that bothers you, but the contrast with the surrounding darkness. In bright sunlight, the same light would be only a dim glow.

You can destroy the effect of light in one place if there's too much in another. The modeling of a smaller-foliaged plant at the base of a tree will be lost if the tree itself is dramatically floodlighted.

When a room is lighted and it is dark outside the glass, the glass will reflect the room lights as a mirror would. You can cut down this reflection by adding light outside and reducing it inside. It takes relatively little light outside to reduce all

Backlighting from below is dramatic because it seldom occurs in nature. It is best on translucent leaves.

Silhouetting shows shape and outline of plant, is best used with bold forms. Panel behind plant is lighted.

Shadows are striking by-product of light. Here, the shadow on panel is more decorative than plant.

Close-up of garden shown on page 81 shows how four buried lamps on a low-voltage lighting system can add interest and depth to plant material.

Dramatic form of tropical plants is accented by a weather-proof metal fluorescent lighting fixture on the ground. Garden design: W. Bennett Covert.

Facial tissues, white glue, and colored yarn molded around balloons make these lights supported by extension cords.

A garden bench provides an opportunity for a light like this. Under this bench in *Sunset's* patio, two 18-inch fluorescent lights are fastened under each of two bench sections. Note light on flower bed.

Lily pad reflectors softly illuminate this garden pool. These come with waterproof cord and socket. Electricity in water can be dangerous, so get the best waterproof cord and socket you can.

Walnut tree with branches backlighted from below. Trunk is silhouetted against board fence.

reflections except those coming from a bright direct light. You can experiment with lights inside and out until you get a balance that virtually eliminates reflection on your windows.

In all garden lighting, experimenting pays off. Try out your ideas before you install any permanent wiring or fixtures.

In working with extension cords for temporary lighting, remember that grass is usually wet at night and a shock could be fatal. Use all waterproof cords, outlets, and fixtures. It is safest to screw in lamps and plug in extensions when the switch is off. Make all your connections and adjustments first; then turn the switch.

PERMANENT INSTALLATIONS

Wiring for a permanent garden lighting system should be buried underground. Any electrical system is potentially dangerous; an outdoor system needs a special installation if it is to be safe.

When you start, check first with your electrical inspector to see what materials are approved in your community and what kind of inspection is required for garden wiring. Local practice and electrical code requirements vary a good deal from town to town. In some areas all underground wiring must be in rigid metal conduit. In others you can use the less expensive direct burial cable.

If you plan to do your own wiring, you will usually need a permit and the inspector will check your work. If you use direct burial cable, it may need extra protection. You can lay it under header boards or along the edge of a path where you aren't likely to hit it with a shovel.

In areas where you might be digging, it is a good idea to fasten the cable to the bottom of a redwood or cedar 1 by 2 and bury it under the board for protection.

Use No. 14 wire for runs of less than 100 feet and a load of up to 1,500 watts. Use No. 12 wire

Japanese lanterns make wonderful party lights. They are inexpensive, colorful, gay, and festive. These are fastened to a string of outdoor Christmas lights.

To make this fixture, you lace a 4-foot square of perforated aluminum into a circle and set it over photo reflector. Edges are lapped, laced with wire.

for runs over 100 feet and 2,000 watts.

Dig the trench 14 to 18 inches deep, put sand or fine soil in the bottom to protect the cable and lay it in place. Cover it after the electrical inspector has checked the connections.

Use conduit where the cable comes out of the ground. The conduit keeps the cable from chafing at this critical point, and it also provides a support for outlet boxes.

If you plan to use outdoor electrical outlets for electric garden tools, the outlets should be grounded as a safety precaution. Use thin wall metal tubing to keep wires you run up into a tree from chafing as the tree moves.

LOW VOLTAGE LIGHTING EQUIPMENT

This kind of lighting equipment makes it possible to install garden lighting safely, relatively inexpensively (much of the saving is in installation cost), and without the need for a building permit. This equipment is also easier to install than a 110-volt wiring system in an established garden.

Low voltage does not mean low light. You get a great deal of light from automobile headlights at 12 volts, but because that is low voltage, you can't get a shock.

To install the system, you need an electric outlet for the transformer and a housing to conceal and protect it from weather. Connect the cable and lead it out into the garden. (Bury it under an inch or so of soil when the lights are placed, but mark the line so you don't cut it with a spade.) Connect lights anywhere on the cable by slitting the cable for 3 inches, pressing it into grooves in the lamp bottom, and screwing on the cap. You can easily relocate lamps. Position them by partially burying them in the ground or attaching them to spikes.

A package of transformer, 100 feet of plastic-coated cable, 6 reflector lamps (with a choice of 6 colors or clear plastic lenses), and 6 spikes costs about $87. Six extra lamps and 100 extra feet of cable will operate on the same transformer.

With 12 lamps, the system draws 150 watts and will not overload most household circuits. At nominal cost you can buy 3-prong grounded adapter plugs to fit the transformer plug to a 2-prong outlet, and connections so you can lay out branch lines off a main line.

Low-voltage lighting equipment is used here to dramatize a small entry garden designed by John Carmack. System is easy to install, and because it uses little current, you can't get a shock.

Standard outdoor lighting fixture marks the edge of a parking area and corner of path leading to entry. Garden design: Lawrence Halprin.

Mugho pine, floodlighted from below, appears as a magnificent burst of light. Its dense growth blocks glare even when it is viewed close up.

Delicate tracery of Japanese maple is silhouetted against battened wall. Light source is torpedo fixture. Louver is used to cut glare from above.

Light from below casts shadows on board-and-batten wall and creates indirect light on soffit above. Design: Eckbo, Royston & Williams.

Floodlighted garden shows another way to handle light. Here, the garden at night has much the same character, form, and color as it has by day. It becomes a continuation of the house itself, and the beauty of the garden replaces drawn draperies or cold black windows. Garden design: Chuck Ito.

CLYDE CHILDRESS

Floodlight is screened by potted daffodils and cyclamen clustered around its base. Back lighting on flowers casts pleasing shadow patterns.

BLAIR STAPP

Photographer's floodlight, directed toward the underside of beach umbrella, casts a wide circle of soft light above the patio table.

WILLIAM APLIN

Lighted plant outside window gives soft light as restful setting for quiet conversation inside the room. Garden design: W. Bennett Covert.

ERNEST BRAUN

Flare pots edge circular walk outside living room window. Water from hose keeps pavement wet so flame is reflected. Garden is floodlighted so there is no reflection in windows. Garden design: Douglas Baylis.

DEARBORN-MASSAR

Lighted candles—the short, stubby variety—floating in small bird bath along with a single camellia blossom look festive when they're placed near an entrance at night.

ERNEST BRAUN

Candles on fence are supported on nails. To protect fence, you could make a sconce from coffee can lid: Bend lid through center to form right angle. Half of lid supports candle, other half protects fence.

LIGHTING WITH FLAME

The flickering warm color of flame is exciting in the garden at night. The lighting on these two pages requires no wiring.

The biggest flame you can get, and one of the most satisfying, is the blazing bonfire. The one shown on the opposite page is contained in a big cast-iron bucket.

The funnel-shaped *luau* torches have a festive South Sea Islands air. The auto flares in the pictures above and opposite work very well. They are compact, easy to store, and burn for 8 to 12 hours without refilling.

You can make a flare pot by simply cutting a hole in the top of a coffee can or screw-top jar and putting a heavy wick through into the kerosene in the container. Keep kerosene-burning torches downwind and away from the house to avoid the black smelly smoke.

Candles can be lovely used in mass, or where you can see them up close.

Hawaiian luau torch, mounted on bamboo pole, burns common kerosene, provides a darting flame that lights up background of olive tree branches.

Above. Bonfire in iron bucket gives light and heat on patio. Fire can be moved from one spot to another depending on climate.

Left. Fire and water make a dramatic combination. These are kerosene-burning flare pots designed for use as safety flares for motorists.

DECORATING WITH LIGHT   85

CHARLES W. TOTTEN

Glass cylinder with candle inside is supported by a ring welded to the vertical wires. Cross wires support can lid which holds candle.

GARDEN LIGHT THAT HANGS IN A TREE

This garden lantern is a kind of rugged version of a Japanese lantern. You make it with coat hanger wire, 3 metal rings, and a cylinder of glass.

Shop first for the cylinder of translucent glass. The one shown in the photograph is 10 inches long and 5 inches in diameter; it was purchased at a surplus store. You might substitute a clear glass lamp chimney or a piece of glass tubing. If you wish, glue translucent plastic, like that used for making lamp shades, to the outside.

Bend pieces of coat hanger wire, or wire of about the same gauge, to form a cage for the glass cylinder. Cut a shorter piece of wire to make the top loop for hanging the lantern. Cut out the bottom of a large tin can to go inside the glass cylinder.

Then take the cage to a welding shop. Buy two rings about 2 inches in diameter for the top and bottom of the lantern, and a third larger ring to support the glass cylinder. The middle ring should have one or more lengths of wire across it. Have only the two bottom rings welded in place; you will want to remove the top ring to replace the candle.

Design: John Keal.

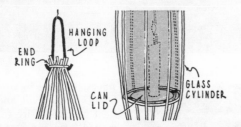

Left. Sketch shows details of lantern pictured above. Make slight hook at both ends of each piece of wire to fit inside the end rings.

CLYDE CHILDRESS

A tin can, candle, and a hammer and nail are all it takes to make this sparkling bit of whimsey. It gives light, and will also keep coffee warm.

ERNEST BRAUN

Soft candlelight shines through patterned sheet plastic. Tack and glue plastic to ¾-inch plywood base; glue seam, then glue on veneer strips.

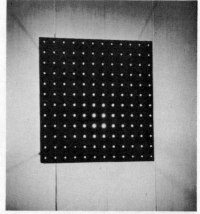

CLYDE CHILDRESS

Perforated hardboard makes sparkling pattern in front of a light. The shadows against wall are made by dowels supporting the panel.

Strong plant and structural forms of this garden make it especially suited to night lighting. Torpedo fixture on ground is shielded by planter, left; in center, unshielded PAR lamp is screened by plants in bed; lamp on ground behind fence, right, backlights plants, screen. An unshielded lamp is mounted out of sight in eave to left, and there are two torpedo fixtures in tree, right. Design: Kathryn Stedman.

Japanese paper parasol makes colorful party light in front of a bare bulb. Handle of parasol is held in a hole bored in the fence.

Food graters. placed over candles, make a delightful pattern of light. The varied hole sizes and louvered top (potato cutter) add more interest.

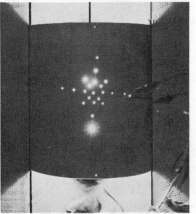

Pierced tin sheet, bent to half cylinder, fits spaces between fence boards. Lapped-over ends of sheet metal and wiring are secured to rear of fence.

Light from a 60-watt bulb in Chinese lantern is augmented by 150-watt floodlight mounted under the eaves, out of sight from the living room.

Bright light shines downward, soft glow upward. This light illuminates steps in the entry between carport and house. Design: John Lloyd Wright.

Copper flower-shaped bells light this garden bed bordering entry walk. Light behind fence shines through to add a vertical pattern.

Indirect, diffused light comes from lamp mounted on fence. Light emphasizes contrasting forms of purple leaf plum at right, New Zealand flax plant, left.

Sheet copper, bent into semi-circular shields and mounted on post gives good indirect light from common light bulbs.

Shielded, louvered floodlight shines down through leaves and branches of oak tree. Gallon jug on corner of the raised pool is novel candle holder: bottom was removed, top mounted in cork disc. Design: Henry Hill.

Graceful elm and bed of primroses below it are lighted by clamp-on units placed in the open grill of overhead. Design: Eckbo, Royston & Williams.

Two glass blocks, with a light bulb below, replace an adobe brick to light an aralia in corner of planting bed next to house.

DECORATING WITH LIGHT 89

Your guests arrive. Giant 6-foot paper parasols, stuck in 20-gallon reed-wrapped cans filled with sand, are lighted from beneath to extend a cheerful invitation to arriving guests. Parasols are Japanese, come in many colors.

Decorating for a Party

With a little stage managing, you can turn any garden into a party world. You are bounded only by your imagination, your lot lines, and the sky.

All of the garden props and settings shown on these pages are temporary, calling for no permanent construction or improvements, and no big expense. The ideas themselves touch on the South Seas, moonlight and stardust, and the supernatural. Yet behind the web of fabrication, you'll find some easy-does-it party planning and a host of practical short cuts and ideas.

The out-of-doors, especially after dark, calls for exaggerated size and color. To stand out against the sky, trees, and houses, an outdoor decoration must be insistent and conspicuous. The bigger, the brighter, the bolder, the better!

Even in the most generous garden area, guests will cluster together unless you give them good reason to move around. Big-size outdoor decorations help—pinned high and low, nearby and in the distance. The lure of food also helps to keep people moving—a crisp, cold bite here, a real, hunger-satisfying buffet over there. The whole idea is to spread things out—dancing, food, drinks, games—each in a different part of the garden.

Daytime logic doesn't belong to a nighttime party. Instead of relying on specific and expected accessories, such as paper favors and flower decoration, try to capture the party qualities themselves—color, movement, excitement, coolness, warmth. As you do, beach towels become 3-by-6-

foot areas of floating color, aluminum foil becomes glint and reflections and crinkling noise, fire becomes flickering light and shadow.

Make your driveway a party entry by setting up a temporary shield between carport and street. This you can make using reed or bamboo matting, cloth, or cardboard, with poles and wire. The shield in our photograph at left is reed matting secured with a wire stretched from house wall to a property line fence. The carport or garage becomes an arrival lanai or arrival patio, serves later as one of two major outdoor areas (the other is your regular terrace or patio).

The imported Japanese parasols in the photograph are useful in many ways: as shade for an afternoon party; as light reflectors at night (shine a floodlight from the ground onto the underside of the parasol); as a canopy for your serving cart (see photograph at right). Or you can use lawn or beach umbrellas to suggest the gay atmosphere of a sidewalk cafe.

You can work wonders with ice and dry ice. Try stringing ice cubes with holes to make an ice screen (the cubes are available by the sack

Giant sized decorations: Plastic beach balls suspended from beams, giant cardboard butterfly on fence, 7-foot flying fish (poster-painted on wrapping paper, two sides edge-glued, stuffed with crumpled newspaper).

Garden party light is a cluster of colorful dime-store balloons fastened to a tree and lighted from below by a 150-watt floodlight bulb.

Child's wagon forms base for patio service cart. Upper part is wire mesh on wood frame, with plywood tray top. Into mesh go fatsia leaves, daisies (see photo above).

Garden table can be quickly converted into a tropical canopied buffet. Use bamboo poles (or light lumber or peeled poles) for uprights, reed matting (or canvas) for canopy. Hanging decorations are pasted paper.

from some ice companies and liquor stores). Cubes last longer if deep frozen at 0° for a few hours before they are used.

Ice sculpture isn't really easy, but it's fun, and results are often surprising. Get 150-pound cakes from an ice company. Use an ice pick (cautiously), wood rasp, or a light hatchet.

Flame offers an easy, cheerful, and highly decorative basis for party lighting. If your nights are chilly, you can set up a flaring log fire in a firepit or bucket; supplement it with the glow of charcoal in braziers. Torches make excellent party lights. So do candles, but they usually will need wind protection. Put sand in the bottom of open paper sacks and stick candles in the sand. Use the sacks to line your entry; mount them on patio tables, on the top of fence posts. Or use glass hurricane lamp chimneys or cylindrical sec-

tions of plastic. Glance through pages 76 through 89 for more ideas for temporary garden lighting.

Imagination is the most essential ingredient when you decorate the garden for a party. Using it, there is no end to the things you can convert to frivolous party purposes. Sometimes obvious helps are overlooked. Your portable barbecue, minus its grill, will make an efficient patio heater-brazier. A lawn sprinkler tape on the roof edge or fence top sets up a cooling "rain." Tree trunks change character with spiral candy stripes in red and white crepe paper. What do these materials suggest to you? A roll of wrapping paper, poster paint, or spray paint in aerosol cans. Some Navajo rugs. Fish net. Inflatable water toys. An inflatable wading pool and some giant dahlias. Look around your garage, attic, the children's rooms—the materials are there; all that's needed is your imaginative eye to transform them.

Bright spot in garden is basket lined with sheet of plastic and filled with water, fishing floats, Shasta daisies, and dry ice (renew ice every half hour).

On a high wire strung from house eaves to boards nailed to the property line fence, you can float colorful beach towels for shade, hang decorations, suspend lights.

Serving table holds crushed ice for vegetables on top, flowers below.

Glowing charcoal briquets in hardware cloth cylinder hang from a tree.

"Trees" are painted wood blocks that wave back and forth on steel rods.

Portable dance floor of 4-by-8-foot tempered hardboard panels screwed to a 1-by-4 lumber frame. Floor can be reused or the materials salvaged for other projects.

Solid base for portable floor is patio paving. Floor won't hurt lawn for short periods, but slight wobbliness may be disconcerting. (Stiffer frame would correct this.)

Christmas music—with white porcelain Japanese wind bells. From 1½ to 4 inches in diameter, bells hang from branches on black nylon thread, dangle gold paper strips from clappers. Japanese split bamboo bird cage is full of white cotton birds (weatherproof birds with plastic spray), has small Christmas tree lights inside. Floodlight illuminates scene. Decorations on this page, and pavilion on page 95, by landscape architect Roy Rydell.

Christmas Decorating Ideas

Here are ingenious and refreshing ways to express the spirit of Christmas in your garden or at your entry. We might add that the display above, and the lamps at left, would make attractive decorations for an outdoor party at any time of year. The chapters on *Decorating with Light* and *Decorating for a Party* contain a number of ideas that can be adapted to the Christmas garden.

Most of the materials used here are waterproof. Glass fiber and polyethylene, used in several of the decorations, won't absorb moisture; however, you should coat papier-mâché objects with a plastic spray if you expose them to the weather.

Black ceramic Mexican hurricane lamps, adorned with cupids and birds, light steps. Aluminum foil cups catch candle drip. Cherubs on wall have gold tape halos.

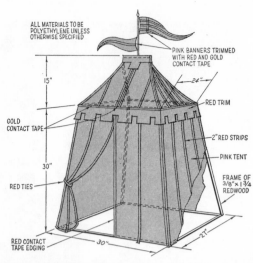

ALL MATERIALS TO BE
POLYETHYLENE UNLESS
OTHERWISE SPECIFIED

PINK BANNERS TRIMMED
WITH RED AND GOLD
CONTACT TAPE

15"

24"

RED TRIM

GOLD
CONTACT TAPE

2" RED STRIPS

PINK TENT

30"

FRAME OF
3/8" x 1 3/4
REDWOOD

RED TIES

RED CONTACT
TAPE EDGING

30"

27"

DARROW M. WATT

Weatherproof pavilion made with soft pink polyethylene, trimmed with red strips on roof and sides, creates setting for Nativity scene. Pink glass fiber forms carpet (handle with rubber or plastic gloves, and take care not to get pieces in eyes). Polyethylene burns on contact with high heat, so light pavilion by hanging small, low-watt bulb inside to give soft glow. Materials used: 13 pieces ⅜ by 1¾-inch redwood, 8 feet long; ¼ pound 2-penny flat head galvanized nails; contact cement for wood joints; 3 yards pink polyethylene, 52 inches wide; 1¾ yards red polyethylene, 52 inches wide; staples and cellophane tape to hold polyethylene to frame.

BLAIR STAPP

GLENN CHRISTIANSEN

Perforated aluminum trees on garden stake trunks are completely weatherproof. Hang outdoor lights inside, or spotlight trees.

Iron stand used to display African violets can be converted to a candle tree. For holiday use, add holly or other greenery around glasses holding candles.

Hoops, suspended by guy wires from broomstick trunk, are decorated with plastic leaves and flowers and base metal ribbon.

Cloud of pink glass fiber (insulation material), papier-mâché cherubs. Cloud made by gluing glass fiber to a window screen form. Light bulb inside. By Roy Rydell.

A leafless tree can be just as dramatic as an evergreen. Here, colored lights sparkle on a 10-year-old Mission fig and outline its gray sinewy branches.

Balsa wood decorations. Cut 2 of each; cut one in half, glue halves to center of uncut piece. Add lacquer design.

Geometric plant boxes, used here with 3-foot-high spruce in Christmas arrangement, can be used in other patterns later. Boxes are made of finished 1-by-3 redwood with a base of exterior hardboard drilled with drain holes.

Aluminum foil pie pans, cut with scissors; use them alone or as settings for other small ornaments.